A-Level Year 1 & AS

Business

Exam Board: AQA

Revising for Business exams is stressful, that's for sure — even just getting your notes sorted out can leave you needing a lie down. But help is at hand...

This brilliant CGP book explains **everything you'll need to learn** (and nothing you won't), all in a straightforward style that's easy to get your head around.

We've also included **exam-style questions** to test how ready you are for the real thing, along with a section of advice on how to pick up as many marks as possible!

A-Level revision? It has to be CGP!

Published by CGP

Editors:
Rob Harrison, Shaun Harrogate, Sharon Keeley-Holden, Ali Palin, Caley Simpson and Ben Train.

Contributors:
Paul Brockbank, Angela Duffy, Peter Gray, Jeff Harris, Adrian Murray, John Evans-Pritchard, Tom Reilly and Keith Williamson.

ISBN: 978 1 78294 352 5

With thanks to Victoria Skelton and Jonathan Wray for the proofreading.
With thanks to Jan Greenway and Laura Jakubowski for the copyright research.

Cover photo © iStockphoto.com/Pinkypills

Clipart from Corel®
Printed by Elanders Ltd, Newcastle upon Tyne.

Based on the classic CGP style created by Richard Parsons.

Contents

We deliberately haven't included answers to most of the questions — that's because there are lots of valid ways to give your answers. Instead, we've put in a section on how to write answers and do well. Answers to numerical questions are included though, on pages 106-107.

Why Businesses Exist

Here's a bit of background for you. You'd be hard-pushed to get as far as your A-levels and not have some idea about why businesses exist, but there's still quite a lot to learn. Here's the basics to get you started.

Businesses Supply **Goods** or **Services**

1) Businesses sell **products** to customers who are willing to **pay** for them. Products can be **goods** or **services**. Goods are **physical items** like books or furniture, whereas services are actions performed by other **people** to aid the customer, e.g. hairdressers and plumbers provide services.

2) Some businesses sell **necessities** — goods or services that you **need** (like gas and electricity). Others provide **luxury** goods or services — things you **want** but don't need (like holidays and jewellery).

There are **Advantages** to owning a **Business**

1) People set up businesses mainly to make a **profit**. This means the business **makes** more money than it **spends**. Starting a business is risky, but many people take the risk because of the possibility of big **financial rewards**.

> A person who starts their own business is called an <u>entrepreneur</u>. Entrepreneurs have to find resources and organise activities needed to start the business.

2) People usually only set up their own business if they expect to make **more** than they could earn working as an **employee** of another company.

3) People may set up their own business so that they can be **their own boss** and make their own decisions — they don't have to answer to anyone else.

4) Setting up your own business also gives you the opportunity to do a job you're really **interested** in.

Most Businesses **Need** to make a **Profit**

1) Businesses have to **make a profit** or **break even** (see p.78) to survive.

2) This is especially true in the **private sector** — if a business doesn't make enough money to survive it could go **bankrupt** and have to **close down**.

> Public sector = government-owned
> Private sector = privately owned

3) In the **public sector**, it's not as clear-cut. Organisations like the army, the police, hospitals and state schools aren't there to **make money** — they provide a service to the community.

4) **Non-profit** businesses, e.g. charities, have **social** or **ethical aims**, rather than financial ones.

> For more on these different forms of business, see p.8.

Businesses can have **Other Aims**

As well as making a profit, businesses may have **other aims**, such as:

- To offer the **highest quality** goods and services possible.
- To give excellent **customer service**.
- To have a great **image** and **reputation**.
- To **develop new products** ahead of competitors.
- To offer a **diverse** range of goods or services.
- To become fully **sustainable** or minimise **environmental impact**.
- To invest in the **local community** or **social projects**.

Geraldine was taking this whole 'aims' thing a bit too literally.

Businesses set specific **objectives** to help them meet their aims, as you'll see over the next few pages.

<u>Don't make all your private sector thoughts too public...</u>

There aren't any questions on this page, but don't let that fool you — there are plenty on the next topic. The most important thing to remember is that, usually, the main aim of a business is to make a profit. However, this isn't always the case. How businesses go about achieving their aims... well, that's a story for the next few pages...

Mission, Aims and Objectives

*The mission, aims and objectives of a business are really important — they're what the
business wants to achieve. They're so important that you've got three pages on them.*

Mission Statements tell you about a Business's Intentions

1) The **mission** of a business is its **overall purpose** or **main corporate aims**.
The **mission statement** is a written **description** of these aims. Mission statements
are intended to make all **stakeholders** aware of what the business does and why,
and to **encourage** all employees to **work towards** its aims.

Stakeholders are people who have an interest in a business (see p.24-25).

2) Mission statements tell you the **purpose** of the business and include other information, such as
its **values**, its **standards**, its **strategy**, who the **customers** are and what makes the business **unique**.

3) Mission statements give clues about the company's **beliefs**. For example, a mission statement that
mentions **ethics** and **principles** gives a big hint that **ethical practice** is important as well as **profitability**.

4) Mission statements can give staff a sense of **shared purpose**, and encourage them to work towards **common
goals** — having the **cooperation** of all the staff makes it more likely that a business will achieve its aims.

5) On the other hand, companies **don't** have to prove that what they say in their mission statement is **accurate**,
so they can say what they think consumers want to hear, without having to do anything about it.
However, this is **bad practice**, and a business's **reputation** will be **damaged** if customers find that its actions
don't reflect its stated values.

Businesses set Objectives at Different Levels

1) Businesses set **objectives** to enable them to achieve their mission.
Objectives turn the overall aims of a business into **specific goals** that must be met.

2) The diagram on the right shows the hierarchy of objectives.
They can be set at the **corporate** or **functional** level.

**Mission Statement
and Corporate Aims**
↓
Corporate Objectives
↓
Functional Objectives

Corporate objectives

Corporate objectives are the goals of the business as a **whole**. The corporate objectives will
depend on the **size** of the business. A new shop owner might focus on trying to **survive**,
while a big international company will want to **grow bigger** and **diversify** its product range.

Functional objectives

Functional objectives (sometimes called **departmental objectives**) are the objectives of
each **department**. They're more **detailed** than corporate objectives, and they are **specific** to
each department. Businesses need to set **functional objectives** that will help them **achieve**
their **corporate objectives**. Whenever a corporate objective is set, **all** the managers in the
business have to look at how their department can help to achieve the objective, and set
functional objectives that will **contribute** to achieving the corporate objective.

3) Businesses set objectives for lots of reasons. If an objective is agreed upon, managers can make
sure that **everyone** is working towards a **goal**, and **coordination** between departments should improve.
Working towards an objective can also be **motivating** for employees. Objectives are really useful
in **decision-making**, as they make it easier to see what the business is trying to achieve.

4) Managers can **compare performance** with their objectives to **measure** the success
of the business and **review** their decisions.

Employees may have their own Personal Objectives

1) Functional objectives **aren't** the last stage of setting objectives — **team managers** within a
department might set objectives for their **team** based on the functional objectives of the whole
department and **individual staff members** might even have their own **personal objectives**.

2) E.g. if the sales department has a functional objective to increase sales by 10% over 12 months,
the telesales team might have an objective to increase sales from 500 to 550 a week.
A telesales operative's objective might be to increase their sales from 20 to 25 a day.

Mission, Aims and Objectives

Objectives should be Specific, Measurable, Agreed, Realistic and Timely

To be effective, a functional objective should be 'SMART' — specific, measurable, agreed, realistic and timely.

<u>S</u>pecific   **Vague objectives** like "to improve quality" **don't** really tell staff what they're supposed to be aiming for. Making them more **specific**, e.g. "to reduce the number of items produced that have defects", means that the business is more likely to **achieve** them.

<u>M</u>easurable   If the objective **isn't measurable**, the business **won't know** if it's achieved it or not. E.g. "to increase profit by 5%" is a measurable objective, but "to improve the business" isn't.

<u>A</u>greed   Everyone who's going to be involved in **achieving** the objective needs to **know** about it and **agree** to it. E.g. if the objective is to increase sales, the sales manager and salespeople will all need to agree to it.

<u>R</u>ealistic   There's no point setting objectives that are **too ambitious**, e.g. tripling sales within 12 months, or achieving a 95% market share. **Impossible objectives** just **demotivate** staff.

<u>T</u>imely   There should be a **specific timeframe** that the objective has to be achieved in. E.g. the objective might be to increase revenue by 5% within 12 months. If there's **no time limit**, staff won't see the objective as **urgent** — they might think they don't need to worry about achieving it because as long as it gets done at some time in the future then it doesn't matter.

Buying a magical thinking cap won't make you SMART.

There are Different Types of Objectives

Businesses will have different objectives, but here are some common ones:

Profit Objectives

1) **Businesses** that are currently making a loss might aim to become **profitable**. Established businesses that are already profitable might want to **increase** their profits, e.g. by 10% within three years.

2) To achieve its overall profit objective, a business may set **functional** objectives to **minimise costs**, which could be an objective for all departments, or to **increase sales**, which could be an objective for the sales and marketing departments.

See pages 6-7 for more information on profit.

Growth Objectives

1) Many businesses aim to grow. The larger a business grows, the more it is able to use its position in the market to earn higher profits.

2) Growth objectives can be based on increasing **revenue**, **market share**, or **expanding** a business.

Survival Objectives

1) Survival just means that a business can continue to trade, rather than running out of **money** or being forced to exit the market for another reason.

2) Survival is often the main objective for **new** businesses, and it becomes a **key objective** during periods of strong competition from other companies, or when the economy is declining or in a recession.

Cash Flow Objectives

1) Cash flow is the money that moves **in** and **out** of a business over a set period of **time**.

2) Businesses set cash flow objectives in order to **improve** their cash flow — i.e. to make sure they always have enough money to make the payments that are due.

3) **Increasing cash flow** gives the company a greater chance of **survival**.

4) There's more on cash flow objectives on p.68 and methods of improving cash flow on p.72-73.

Mission, Aims and Objectives

Social and Ethical Objectives are Important too

1) **Social** objectives relate to benefiting society or people in need. **Ethical** objectives are based on **moral principles** about how businesses treat people and the environment. E.g. principles of fair trade and minimising environmental damage.

2) **Non-profit** organisations, like charities or social enterprises, are set up to achieve social or ethical objectives. E.g. housing associations provide affordable housing for people on low incomes.

3) **For-profit** businesses usually focus on making a **profit**. However, social and ethical objectives are becoming increasingly important, especially as information on how businesses operate is becoming more widely **available**. Businesses might set objectives to provide **facilities** for the local community, or to only buy from suppliers who pay a **fair** wage. People are more likely to buy from a business with good ethical practices, which can help achieve other aims too.

Marks & Spencer successfully made their UK business carbon neutral by setting a number of ethical objectives.

Businesses can have Short-term and Long-term Objectives

1) **Long-term** objectives include things like long-term growth. **Long-term objectives** tend to set the **direction** of a business. They affect the **big decisions** that senior managers make.

2) **Short-term** objectives include things like short-term **survival** and making short-term **profit**, but they often require a business to cut back on its long-term objectives.

3) For example, a business trying to increase on last year's profits might **cut** its **advertising** budget, stop its **training** programme, and cut back on its **product development** budget. At the end of the year it'd have **more profit** because of cutting all those **costs**, but it would have lost out on its other objectives.

4) Businesses are often **criticised** for being too concerned with **short-term gain**. Shareholders often want a **quick return** on their investment, or they'll take their money and go elsewhere. Businesses have to go for short-term profits or risk losing investors.

5) There needs to be a good **balance** between long-term and short-term objectives.

Practice Questions

Q1 Give three examples of information that could be included in a mission statement.

Q2 What is the difference between a corporate objective and a functional objective?

Q3 Give two examples of corporate objectives. For each corporate objective, write down two functional objectives that would help the business to achieve it.

Q4 What does SMART stand for in the term 'SMART objectives'?

Exam Questions

Q1 Explain what a mission statement is, and discuss why businesses see mission statements as valuable. [4 marks]

Q2 Explain the importance of the SMART criteria for setting objectives. [6 marks]

Mission Statement Impossible — I think I saw that at the cinema...

Ok, so it might not be the most exciting part of Business, but this is really important stuff. The stuff about mission statements is quite good anyway — you can just imagine the scene in the boardroom: "Your mission, if you choose to accept it, is to provide quality sofas and dining furniture." Anyway, your mission is to learn these three pages.

Revenue, Costs and Profit

Profit is the most important objective for many businesses. To measure profit, you'll need to understand revenue and costs, and know how they're calculated. Here's a couple of pages to fill you in on the details.

Revenue is the Money a business makes from Sales

1) Revenue is the **value of sales** — it's sometimes just called **sales** and can also be called **turnover**. It's the amount of money generated by sales of a product, **before** any deductions are made.

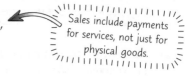
Sales include payments for services, not just for physical goods.

2) You can work out the revenue by multiplying the **price** that the customer pays for each unit by the **number of units** that the business sells:

> **Revenue = selling price per unit × quantity of units sold**

E.g. if a business sells 2000 teapots for £8 each, the revenue is **£8 × 2000 = £16 000**.

3) **Revenue** is affected by both **sales volume** and **price**. If sales volume increases by 50%, revenue will increase by 50%. Increasing the selling price may increase the revenue, but it depends on what effect the higher price will have on the number of sales — see **price elasticity of demand** on p.36-37.

Costs can be Fixed or Variable

1) **Fixed costs** don't change with output. **Rent** on a factory, business **rates**, **senior managers' basic salaries** and the cost of **new machinery** are fixed costs. When output increases, a business makes more use of the facilities it's already got. The **cost** of those facilities **doesn't change**.

2) **Variable costs** rise and fall as output changes. Hourly **wages**, **raw material costs** and the **packaging costs** for each product are all variable costs.

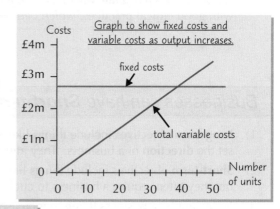

> **Total variable costs = variable cost per unit × number of units sold**

3) **Semi-variable costs** have fixed and variable parts. **Telephone bills** are a good example of **semi-variable** costs. Businesses have to pay a **fixed** amount for their phone line plus a **variable** amount depending on the phone calls they've made.

4) The **total costs** are just the fixed costs plus the variable costs: **Total costs = fixed costs + variable costs**

Profit is the Difference between Revenue and Costs

1) When you deduct the total costs from the total revenue, you're left with the **profit**.

> **Profit = total revenue – total costs**

Revenue, Costs and Profit were all related.

2) If a business's **total revenue** is **greater** than its total costs, then it will make a **profit**. If the **total costs** are **greater** than the total revenue, then the business will make a **loss**.

> E.g. a teapot business has fixed costs of **£4000** pcm and variable costs of **£4** per teapot. It sells **2000** teapots in one month for **£8** each, so its revenue is **£16 000**.
> Its total variable costs that month are 2000 × £4 = **£8000**, so its total costs are £4000 + £8000 = **£12 000**.
> So the profit is: £16 000 – £12 000 = **£4000**

3) Businesses can do different things with profit. Most businesses **give it to the shareholders** as dividend payments or **re-invest** the profit in new activities. But they could also pay staff bonuses, invest it in a bank, give it to charity, or use it to fund projects in the local community.

4) **Shareholders** often want a **short-term** reward for supporting the business. In the long term, it's often better for the business to hold on to the profit and **re-invest** it in future projects.

There's more on shareholders on p.12-13.

Revenue, Costs and Profit

Large-Scale Production helps keep costs Low

The more a business produces, the **lower** the **cost per unit** produced. This is because the **fixed costs** are **shared out** between **more items**. The best way to show this is with an example:

1) MicroDave make microwave ovens. The **fixed costs** of running MicroDave are £200 000 per year. The **variable costs** of materials and labour are £15 per microwave.
2) If MicroDave make **5000 microwaves a year**, the total production costs are... £200 000 + (£15 × 5000) = £275 000. The **cost per microwave** is £275 000 ÷ 5000 = **£55**.
3) If MicroDave make **20 000 microwaves a year**, the total production costs are... £200 000 + (£15 × 20 000) = **£500 000**. The **cost per microwave** is £500 000 ÷ 20 000 = **£25**.

Businesses use information on Product Costs to Make Decisions

1) Businesses use **costs** information to set the **selling price** of their products and services. They set the price to make sure they'll make a **profit**. (Number of sales × price) – costs = profit.

2) If a business is a "**price taker**" in a very competitive market, it **doesn't have control** of the **selling price** of its products — it takes whatever price the market will pay. Businesses in this situation need accurate **costing** information to work out if it's **profitable** to make and sell a product at all. E.g. farmers have to sell milk, carrots, potatoes, etc. to supermarkets for whatever price the supermarkets are willing to pay — if they try to put their prices up, supermarkets will just buy from other farmers instead.

3) Businesses set **budgets** (see p.74-77) which forecast how much costs are going to be over a year. Managers need to monitor costs so that they know whether they're **meeting** the budget.

Profit is Important for Many Reasons

1) **Profit can motivate people** — People in the business who own shares will receive a portion of the profit as a dividend payment (see p.10). Some businesses offer a profit-sharing scheme, where employees are given bonuses from a share of the total profits.

2) **Profit is a good source of finance** — Profit can be retained in the business and used for investments. This can help the business grow and increase profits. Businesses do not need to pay interest on retained profit, like they do with loans, nor does it need to be paid back in the future.

3) **Profit can be used to attract investors** — Potential investors look at profit levels when deciding whether to buy shares in a company. People are more likely to invest if a business is making a large profit, as they'll expect a good dividend payment.

For more on profits, go to p.70-71.

Practice Questions

Q1 What is the formula for calculating revenue?
Q2 Give three examples of fixed costs.
Q3 Why is profit important? Give three reasons.

Answers on p.106.

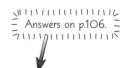

Exam Questions

Q1 Bricks 'n' More Tar Co. has a revenue of £650 000 in one year. Their fixed costs are 23% of the revenue, and their total variable costs are 54% of the revenue. Calculate the profit made by Bricks 'n' More Tar Co. [3 marks]

Q2 Beth Brook Hats employs two hat-makers, each at £280/week. Beth, as Managing Director, pays herself £400/week. The other fixed costs are £300/week. The variable costs of raw materials are £14 per hat. Hats sell for £50.

a) Draw a graph to show fixed, variable and total costs for outputs from 0 hats/week to 100 hats/week. [6 marks]
b) Calculate the profit that Beth is making at her current output level of 60 hats per week, assuming weekly sales match output. [4 marks]

If you don't learn this, it'll cost you...

Costs, revenue and profit are pretty simple concepts, but very important ones. They'll crop up in other topics, so make sure you get them straight in your head. You need to be able to calculate revenue and profit, so learn the formulas well, and make sure you're clear on the difference between fixed and variable costs too. Oh joy...

Different Forms of Business

There are loads of different forms of business, and each form has different aims, benefits and drawbacks.
Unfortunately there's only one thing for it — get stuck into these pages and learn them all.

Organisations can be in the *Public Sector* or the *Private Sector*

Public sector organisations are owned and run by the **Government**. They aim to provide services to the public, rather than make a profit. NHS hospitals are one example — their aim is to provide health care that's available to everyone. Organisations like the NHS, UK police forces and the fire service are run in a similar way to other businesses, but they don't charge for their services so don't make a profit — they are funded by the UK **tax system**.

Private sector organisations are owned and run by **private individuals**. They range from small sole traders to huge organisations such as John Lewis and ASDA. Most private sector businesses aim to make a **profit**, however this is not always the case — **non-profit** organisations such as **charities** are also part of the private sector.

Non-Profit businesses have different *Aims* and *Objectives*

1) As their name suggests, non-profit businesses are **not** set up to make a **profit**. Instead, they have other aims, often to **help** people in need or benefit the community. Like other businesses, they usually have money coming **into** and going **out** of the business — the main **difference** is that the money generated by the business **doesn't** go to the owners or shareholders as **profit**.

2) **Charities** like the British Red Cross, Oxfam and Amnesty International make money from **donations** and business activities (like charity shops). This money is used to fund charitable activities, e.g. setting up hospitals in developing countries. Charities get **tax reductions** because of their non-profit structure.

3) **Social enterprises** are normal businesses with a **social objective**. The business **trades** and **makes profit** like any other business, but its profits are used to pay for its **social activities**. E.g. the profits from sales of One® Water bottled water are used to fund clean water projects in villages in Africa.

4) **Mutual organisations** like building societies aim to offer their customers the best possible value on products and services. **Profits** are **reinvested** into the business in order to **reduce prices** — that means that building societies can often offer higher savings rates and lower loan rates than banks, because they don't have to pay any of their profits to shareholders.

Liability to pay off *Business Debts* can be *Limited* or *Unlimited*

Responsibility for **business debts** works differently for different forms of business.

Unlimited liability

1) If a business has unlimited liability, the **business** and the **owner** are **seen as one** under the **law**. This is the case for **sole traders** (see p.9).

2) This means **business debts** become the **personal debts** of the owner. Sole traders can be forced to **sell personal assets** like their **house** to pay off business debts.

3) Unlimited liability is a **huge financial risk** — it's an important factor to consider when deciding on the type of ownership for a new business.

Limited liability

1) Limited liability means that the owners **aren't personally responsible** for the debts of the business.

2) The **shareholders** (owners) of both **private** and **public limited companies** (see p.10) have limited liability, because a limited company has a **separate legal identity** from its owners. The **most** the shareholders in a limited company can lose is the money they have **invested** in the company.

The difference between limited liability and unlimited liability is **really important**. E.g. a builder puts **£1500** into their own business and the business hits bad times, then goes bankrupt, owing **£20 000**. If the owner is a **sole trader**, he or she is liable to pay the **full debt** of **£20 000** (on top of the original £1500 they invested). If they're a **shareholder** of a limited company, they only lose the **£1500** they put in.

Different Forms of Business

Sole Trader Businesses are run by an Individual

1) A sole trader is an **individual** trading in his or her own name, or under a suitable trading name.
   Sole traders are **self-employed**, for example as shopkeepers, plumbers, electricians, hairdressers or consultants.

2) The essential feature of this type of business is that the sole trader
   has **full responsibility** for the **financial control** of his or her own
   business and for meeting **running costs** and **capital requirements**.
   Having full responsibility for all the **debts** of the business is
   called **unlimited liability** (see p.8).

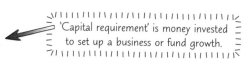
'Capital requirement' is money invested to set up a business or fund growth.

3) There are **minimal legal formalities** — the trader simply has to start trading.
   However, if the business isn't run under the **proprietor's** (owner's) name,
   the trader has to **comply** with certain rules under the Business Names Act (1985).

Being a Sole Trader has Advantages and Disadvantages

There are several **advantages** of being a sole trader:

- **Freedom** — the sole trader is his or her **own boss** and has complete **control** over decisions.
- **Profit** — the sole trader is entitled to **all the profit** made by the business.
- **Simplicity** — there's **less form-filling** than for a limited company. Bookkeeping is less complex.
- **Savings on fees** — there aren't any legal costs for drawing up an ownership agreement.

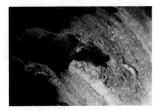
Bears — just another hiccup in Sally's plan to become a sole trader.

There are **disadvantages** too:

- **Risk** — there's **no one** to **share the responsibilities** of running the business with.
- **Time** — sole traders often need to **work long hours** to meet tight deadlines.
- **Expertise** — the sole trader may have **limited skills** in areas such as finance.
- **Finance** — finance is limited to the money that the owner has, or can borrow.
- **Vulnerability** — there's **no cover** if the trader **gets ill** and can't work.
- **Unlimited liability** — the sole trader is **responsible** for all the debts of the business.

Practice Questions

Q1 What is the aim of public sector organisations? How are they funded?

Q2 What do social enterprises use their profits for?

Q3 What's the difference between limited liability and unlimited liability?

Q4 What are the advantages and disadvantages of being a sole trader?

Exam Question

Q1 Peter is a sole trader. Over the last three years he has been making a loss.
If this continues, the business may face bankruptcy. Explain the advantages and
disadvantages to Peter of being a sole trader as he attempts to turn the business around. [6 marks]

Sole traders — they're not just shoemakers...

*...They can also be plumbers, greengrocers... You get the idea. The important thing to remember here is that
sole traders have unlimited liability. If you're going to set up as one, you need to be pretty sure that
your business isn't going to fail or you'll be in big trouble... cos debts don't mind getting personal.*

Different Forms of Business

Companies are different from sole traders. They have limited liability for a start.

There are two kinds of **Limited Liability Companies** — **Ltds** and **PLCs**

1) There are **private limited companies (Ltds)** and **public limited companies (PLCs)**.

2) Public and private limited companies have **limited liability** (see p.8).

3) They're owned by **shareholders** and run by **directors**.

There's more on shareholders on pages 12-13.

4) The **capital value** (or the monetary value) of the company is divided into **shares** — these can be **bought** and **sold** by shareholders. Shareholders have part ownership of a company.

Private Limited Companies	Public Limited Companies
Can't sell shares to the public. People in the company own all the shares.	Can sell shares to the **public**. They usually issue a **prospectus** to inform people about the company before they buy.
Don't have share prices quoted on **stock exchanges**.	Their share prices can be quoted on **stock exchanges**.
Shareholders may not be able to sell their shares without the **agreement** of the **other shareholders**.	Shares are **freely transferable** and can be bought and sold through stockbrokers, banks and share shops.
They're often **small** family businesses.	They usually start as private companies and then **go public** later to raise more capital.
There's **no minimum share capital** requirement.	They need **over £50 000** of share capital, and if they're listed on a stock exchange, **at least 25%** of this must be publicly available. People in the company can own the rest of the shares.
They end their name with the word "limited" or **Ltd**.	They always end their name with the initials **PLC**.

5) The Companies Act (2006) says that several important documents must be drawn up **before** a company can start trading, including the **memorandum of association** and the **articles of association**.

6) These documents must be sent to **Companies House** — where records of all UK companies are kept. The Registrar of Companies issues a **certificate of incorporation** so that the company can start trading. Once it's up and running, the company is legally obliged to produce **annual reports** of its financial activities.

Companies are **Run** by **Directors**

1) In a **small** private limited company, the **directors** are usually the **shareholders** (owners) of the business.

2) In **larger** private limited companies, **directors** are **elected** to the **board** by shareholders. The board makes the important decisions.

3) Shares in a PLC can be owned by **anyone**. The people who **own** the company **don't** necessarily **control** the company — it's controlled by the **directors**. This is called the "divorce of ownership and control".

Ordinary Share Capital is Money raised by Selling Shares

1) Shares are sold by companies to raise money. Money raised in this way is called **ordinary share capital**. Ordinary share capital is usually used for **long-term investment**.

2) In return for their investment, shareholders are paid a **dividend**. Dividends are a **proportion** of the **profits** earned by the company which are split and paid out to the shareholders. Dividends are given as a **fixed amount per share** — the more shares an individual holds, the larger the payout.

3) Dividends aren't always paid out. Loans must be repaid first and a company may choose to re-invest their profits into the business.

4) **Market capitalisation** is the **total value** of all of the ordinary shares **issued** by a company. It is found by multiplying the number of shares issued by the current market price of one share.

Market capitalisation = Number of issued shares × Current share price

E.g. In January 2014 a company issues 25 000 shares for £1 each, so its **ordinary share capital** is **£25 000**. By September 2014, the price of its shares on the Stock Exchange has risen to £4. If all shares are fully paid for, the company's share capital remains at £25 000, but its **market capitalisation** will be 25 000 × £4 = **£100 000**.

Different Forms of Business

Entrepreneurs have to Choose a Legal Structure for their business

1) When someone sets up a business, they have to **decide** what legal structure to set up as. Each structure has **advantages** and **disadvantages** — the entrepreneur has to decide which is most **suitable** for their needs.

2) Setting up a **sole trader** business gives the owner **control** over the business, but **unlimited liability** is a drawback. It's a **simple** way to set up a small business, but there's a lot of **risk** involved for the owner.

3) A **private limited company** has **limited liability** and the shareholders keep **control** over who the other shares are sold to, but it's much more **complicated** to set up than a sole trader business. A new business that needs to invest heavily in equipment, land etc. might need to set up as a Ltd to raise finance.

4) **Public limited companies** aren't usually a suitable option for new businesses because they need at least **£50 000** of share capital to start with, and most new businesses can't raise that much money.

5) Businesses can **change** their structure — sole traders can become a private limited company if the business is successful and they want to expand. This will bring more money and ideas into the business. Lots of private limited companies become PLCs when they want to raise more money to **expand** the business. It's much less common, but PLCs can also become private limited companies if they are taken over by a private limited company or if the managers **buy out** the **shareholders**. For example, in 2002, Arcadia Group PLC was taken over by Philip Green's private limited company Taveta Investments Ltd. and is now Arcadia Group Ltd. PLCs can be changed into Ltds if the original owners want to take more control, or to run things more privately.

Different Forms of Ownership affect the Mission, Objectives and Decisions

1) The **missions** and **objectives** of **non-profit** organisations are usually to help people or communities in need. They will set objectives to generate enough profit to achieve these aims.

2) **Private sector** for-profit organisations often have **objectives** which focus on **maximising** profits, although they will also pursue other objectives (see p.3-5). **Public sector** organisations tend to have missions aimed towards benefiting **society**. This can mean that **social benefits** are put before costs when making decisions.

3) **Sole traders** and owners of small **private limited companies** have **control** over objectives and decision making. They may change ownership if the business is expanding. For sole traders in particular, changing the business to a Ltd company may mean gaining **expertise** from shareholders, however they may not share the same **values** as the original owner, leading to different **objectives** and difficulties when making **decisions**. Shareholders may also buy a large proportion of the shares, meaning the original owner(s) may **lose control** of the business, which may lead to a change in the mission or objectives.

4) For **public limited companies**, the majority of shareholders are not involved in the management of the business. This can lead to a conflict of interests. E.g. management may wish to pursue objectives designed to achieve long-term gains, but which may cause short-term **reductions** in profits. However, they may need to take into account shareholders' wishes for short-term **boosts** to profits.

Practice Questions

Q1 State two differences between private and public limited companies.

Q2 How do you work out the market capitalisation of a business?

Q3 Why are new businesses not usually set up as PLCs?

Exam Question

Q1 Made-Up Organics, a company selling organic make-up and toiletries, is owned by Isabelle Greenberg, a sole trader. The business has been growing over the past few years and she is thinking of becoming a private limited company instead. Explain the advantages and disadvantages of doing this.   [6 marks]

Market capitalisation doesn't mean "MARKET"...

This is all pretty important stuff, so keep reading through until you're confident with all the pros and cons of each form of business. Remember that a Ltd is a private limited company, and a PLC is a public limited company. You should also know how to calculate market capitalisation — number of issued shares × current share price.

The Role of Shareholders

Shareholders invest capital into companies in return for a share of that company. It may sound weird, but that's just the way businesses work. Have a good look at this spread and you'll be a shareholding whizz in no time.

Shareholders are the Owners of Companies

1) A shareholder is anyone who owns at least one share in a company. Shares in a **public limited** company can be bought by **individuals**, **companies** or **institutions** (such as pension funds). Shares in **private limited** companies are usually bought by **family** and **friends** of the original owners.

2) For companies, the main **role** of shareholders is to **provide funds**. In small Ltds, the shareholders are often also the directors of the company — the shareholders with the most shares have the most power. In PLCs, most shareholders are **not** involved in running the business, but they have certain rights.

The Bear Truth PLC's annual general meeting was getting way out of control. Again.

3) Companies hold an **Annual General Meeting** (AGM). Ordinary shareholders have the right to **vote** on key decisions and the performance of the company. Each share that a person holds entitles them to one vote. If a shareholder owns **more than 50%** of the shares, they're called the **majority shareholder**. The majority shareholder has the most **power** in decision-making.

4) Shareholders have the right to receive a **dividend** (a portion of the business's profit), **if** the profit is being used in this way.

5) Shareholders have **limited liability**. If the company can't repay its debts, a shareholder can only lose the money they invested — the amount they spent on shares.

Shareholders Invest in companies for Different Reasons

1) Some shareholders invest in businesses in order to achieve a capital gain. They may buy shares in a business when the share price is low and sell them if the share price rises to make a profit. E.g. an investor purchases 100 shares at £3 each. The share price then rises to £5 each, so the investor sells them at a profit of £2 per share — they gain £2 × 100 = £200.

2) Shareholders may be paid a dividend in return for their investment. Dividends are paid on a per-share basis, so the more shares a shareholder owns, the bigger the dividend.

3) Some people become shareholders because they want to be involved in the running of a business. People may invest in a small private limited company for this reason. A shareholder could influence decision-making in a PLC by buying enough shares to make them the majority shareholder.

4) Some shareholders will invest in a company because they believe in the aims and objectives of the company and want to see it succeed, e.g. companies with social, ethical or environmental objectives.

5) A shareholder might invest in a private limited company in order to help the company survive or grow, e.g. to support a family or friend's company.

The TV show "Dragons' Den" is a good example of venture capital investment. The "Dragons" are professional investors hoping to invest in businesses that will be successful in the future.	6) Venture capitalists are a particular type of shareholder. They will invest in businesses that they think have the potential to be successful (see p.81). This can be a big financial risk but can lead to large financial rewards.

The Role of Shareholders

Share Prices change Constantly

1) **Private limited companies** have **control** over their share price because shares are **privately** traded between friends and family. A price per share will be agreed between the current owner and the potential investor, based on the current performance of the business.

2) Shares in **public limited companies** are sold on the stock market. The price of a company's shares will be determined by **demand and supply**. If more people want to **buy** a share than sell it (demand is higher than supply), the share price goes **up**. If more people want to **sell** a share than buy it (supply is higher than demand), the share price goes **down**.

Factors influencing demand and supply

1) The **performance** of the company — **better performance** should mean bigger dividend payments. This leads to an **increase in demand** for the company's shares, increasing the share price. If a company reports **low profits**, shareholders may **sell** their shares, increasing supply and reducing share price.

2) **Speculation** and rumour of **new product launches** or **cost saving initiatives** might generate investor **interest**. If the rumoured activity is likely to increase the company's profits, this will encourage people to buy shares in the company. As a result, the share price is likely to increase.

3) **Current share price** — if the share price is **low**, investors might think they can get a bargain if they buy now, hoping that the price will increase in the future. If the share price is **high**, shareholders may decide to sell their shares to make a **capital gain**.

4) **Interest rates** — when interest rates are **low**, the reward for saving money in a bank is reduced. This can increase the **demand** for shares because the financial rewards are likely to be **greater** than the **interest** that would be earned on a **bank account**.

5) The **economy** has a strong influence on demand and supply — when the economy is **strong**, people have more money to invest, and **confidence** that they will get a good return. This **increases** demand and share price. In a **weak** economy, people are **less** likely to risk their money on an investment, **decreasing** demand and share price. Businesses may offer **more shares** in order to try and raise share capital, **increasing** supply.

Share Price Changes have Short and Long-Term Effects

1) Changing share prices can have a big effect on shareholders who want to **buy** and **sell** shares for **short-term capital gain**. If the share price **increases**, the shareholder will **make money** when they sell the shares. **Decreasing** share prices may mean a shareholder makes a **loss** when selling shares, or they may decide to hold onto the shares and hope the price **increases** again.

2) Shareholders who buy shares as a **long-term** investment are less affected by **short-term price changes**. However, price changes may reflect an increase or decrease in **company profits**, which could mean **higher** or **lower** dividend payments.

3) A **decrease** in share price can reduce the **overall value** of a company, but in the **short-term** this may not cause too many problems as the business already has the **share capital** — they don't lose it. However, if the share price continues to decrease in the **long-term**, this is likely to **reduce confidence** in the company, making it more difficult to attract **new investors**.

Practice Questions

Q1 Explain who shareholders are.
Q2 Give three possible reasons for buying shares in a business.
Q3 Give two reasons why the share price for a company may decrease.

Exam Questions

Q1 Analyse the effects of a sudden decrease in share price on the shareholders of a company. [6 marks]

Q2 Business Books PLC is a company in the private sector. In 2012 it issued 10 000 shares at a cost of £5.00 each. Between 2012 and 2014, Business Books PLC's profits rose by 35%, and the demand for shares was high. Based on this information, do you think that buying shares in Business Books PLC when they were first issued would have been a good investment? Justify your answer. [12 marks]

Your brain's gonna be in high demand to learn this...

It's not easy stuff, but you will need to learn it all. Read through the pages, then cover them up and scribble down everything you can remember until you know it all. Make sure you understand how demand and supply affect share price — big demand or small supply = prices increase, small demand or big supply = prices decrease.

Businesses and the External Environment

Businesses want demand (the amount of their product that people want to buy) to be high and costs to be low. But this depends on external factors — everything from outside the business that affects it.

Market Conditions affect Costs and Demand

Market conditions is a term that describes a wide range of factors affecting the market. These factors influence the **costs** faced by businesses and the **demand** for their products. They include:

Today's market conditions — mostly sunny, with light showers in the afternoon.

Political Factors

1) If **demand** in the economy is too **low**, governments try to **increase** it. They **cut taxes** so people have **more** to **spend**, and **increase** their **spending** in the economy, for example by raising **benefits**. Central banks (e.g. the Bank of England) **reduce interest rates** to cut mortgage payments and **increase disposable income**.

2) Governments try to **reduce demand** if it's too **high**. They **raise taxes** so people have **less money** to spend, and cut government spending. Central banks **increase interest rates** to raise the cost of **borrowing**, **reduce disposable income** and **reduce demand**.

> Disposable income is your earnings after tax, National Insurance and pension payment have been deducted.

3) The government can also influence demand for **particular** products by using **taxes**. For example, to reduce **carbon emissions**, road tax on **low-emission** and **fuel-efficient cars** has been **reduced**, and road tax on **high-emission** vehicles has been **increased**. **Increased** taxes on products leads to **reduced demand**, as people will try to find cheaper alternatives.

Labour Supply

1) **Labour supply** has an effect on business **costs**.

2) When unemployment rates are **high**, there's a good **supply** of labour. Businesses can hire staff easily and won't have to pay **high wages**, which means costs can be kept low. People in work will be extra **productive** to protect their job.

3) A **low rate** of unemployment could mean that there is a **shortage** of labour. The people available for employment might not have the **skills** needed for the role, so will need **training**. This can **increase costs** for a business.

Incomes and Economic Factors

1) The state of the economy affects **demand** and **costs**. In a **recession**, businesses need to reduce costs, e.g. with **wage cuts** or **redundancies** to decrease labour costs. **Lower incomes** mean people have **less** money to **spend** on products, so **demand decreases**.

2) In an economic **boom**, wages rise and more people are employed. This may lead to **greater costs**, due to the increased wages. On the other hand, **higher incomes** mean that people have more money to spend, **increasing demand** for products. The increased demand leads to **increased production costs** in supplying more products.

3) **Changing incomes** affect demand for **some** products more than others, i.e. depending on whether they are necessities or luxury products. See **income elasticity of demand** on page 37.

Seasonal Demand and Supply

1) There are **variations** in **demand** and **supply** throughout the year. This is called **seasonality**.

2) **Weather** and **holidays** such as Christmas produce variations in **demand**. For example, Christmas creates high demand for toys. Hot weather creates demand for ice lollies, paddling pools and air conditioning units.

3) They can also cause variations in **supply** — for example, more strawberries are available in summer, which would **reduce costs** for a shop selling strawberries.

4) It's impossible to avoid seasonality. Businesses must have **strategies** to deal with it. After Christmas, demand for retail goods drops, so shops **cut prices** (the **January sales**) to boost demand, and get rid of stock.

5) Food producers can cope with seasonality in supply by **preserving food** — e.g. by canning or freeze-drying. This **meets demand** even when the food is not in season.

Competition is another big factor in market conditions. This is covered in more detail on the next page.

Businesses and the External Environment

Competition can Reduce Demand and Increase Costs

When a **competitor** enters the market or launches a new product, the **demand** for a rival business's product is likely to **decrease** as people will buy the competitor's product. The rival business is likely to **increase** its **marketing costs** or spend more on **improving** or **diversifying** its products in response to the competition. Alternatively, the rival might try to **cut** its costs to keep the price of its product lower than the competitor's to **increase demand**.

Different markets have different types of competition between businesses:

1) **Perfect competition** is where all firms compete on an **equal** basis — their **products** are pretty much **identical**, and they all charge a similar price. Businesses need to **keep costs low** to keep prices low, otherwise demand will be taken by the competition. However, they also need to keep a **high quality** of product to keep a good level of demand.

2) In an **oligopoly**, a small number of large firms **dominate** the market and charge similar prices. For a business to get ahead, they will focus on **marketing** and **brand image** to increase demand, so **marketing costs** will be **high**.

3) A **monopoly** is where one business has **complete control** over its market. There's **no competition**. A business with a monopoly can **increase** its **prices** without much concern of the demand decreasing, and they are able to keep **marketing costs low**.

Competition amongst a business's **suppliers** can **reduce costs** for the business.
E.g. if the price of its raw materials decreases.

Interest Rates Determine the Cost of Borrowing Money

1) **Interest rates** affect the **cost of borrowing** and the **return on savings**. The interest rate is the **fee** paid for borrowing — it's calculated as a **percentage** of the amount borrowed. For example, if you borrow £100 with a 10% interest rate, you'll actually pay back £110. A **fall** in interest rates means a **decrease** in the **cost of borrowing** for businesses. A **rise** in interest rates leads to an **increase** in the cost of borrowing.

2) Interest rates affect **consumer spending**. **High interest** rates mean most consumers have **less money** to spend — people with existing **borrowing** (like mortgages) have to pay more money back in **interest**, so they have less **disposable income** (the money left over after essential payments like tax), and so market **demand** goes **down**. People might also decide to **save more** to take advantage of the interest earned on their savings, **reducing demand**. **Low interest** rates mean consumers have more disposable income and there is less reward for saving, so **demand** goes **up**.

3) The effect of interest rates on demand depends on the **product**. Products that require **borrowing** (e.g. cars, houses, kitchens and high-end consumer electronics) are more **sensitive** to interest rate changes. When interest rates go up significantly, firms change strategy to diversify away from these goods and into cheaper ones.

Practice Questions

Q1 Give three factors of market conditions that can affect demand for a product.
Q2 How can high unemployment rates affect a business's costs and demand for its products?
Q3 Why could a new competitor entering the market increase the costs of an existing business?
Q4 How does perfect competition affect business costs and demand for a product?

Exam Questions

Q1 Which of the following could reduce demand for a perfume manufacturer's products? [1 mark]
   A It is December   B High unemployment   C Low interest rates   D A shortage of perfume on the market

Q2 Explain the steps a business could take if a new competitor product enters the market. Describe how this will affect their costs. [6 marks]

I was only showing an interest, now you're trying to charge me for it...

There's heaps of info on these pages, so get your head down and get it learned. You may be asked which factors affect demand and costs and why, so try covering up each chunk and scribble down as many points as you can for each.

Businesses and the External Environment

... But wait, there's more — here we've got demographics, environmental and social factors and technology.
Cast your eyes across these pages. There's lots to learn, but it'll look impressive if you can remember it in your exams.

Businesses have to Respond to Demographic Changes

1) The **structure** of a **population** changes over time in terms of **age**, **sex** and **race** — this is **demographic change**.

2) Demographic change is important to businesses because it has an **impact** on the **demand** for **products**. Different **demographics** of consumers tend to buy **different things**, so businesses need to adapt the **amount** and **type** of products they are **producing**.

3) Demographic changes can mean that **certain types** of business are more **in demand**. This might allow existing businesses to **expand**, or **new businesses** to be set up.

- The UK has an **ageing population** so businesses have started to target the growing elderly market in order to increase demand for their products. E.g. banks have started offering special rates on **retirement accounts** and software developers are making **brain-training games** directed at older people.

- The **ageing population** in the UK has also led to an increased demand for **doctors** and **nurses**, which has increased the **costs** of the NHS (through more treatments and more staff).

- The number of **working parents** is increasing which creates a greater demand for **childcare services**.

- The UK's population is also becoming more **ethnically diverse** as **immigration** levels rise. This has increased demand for certain products, e.g. for food not traditionally available in the UK. Supermarkets have started to stock more **exotic ingredients** and independent 'international' supermarkets have been set up within certain communities.

4) **Consumer tastes** also change over time — in recent years lots more **men** have started using **cosmetic** and **personal grooming** products. Businesses making cosmetic products may adapt them to be more suitable for **different genders** or create a whole **new product range** targeted at men.

The supply of workers affects business costs

1) An ageing population means that a **smaller percentage** of the population are of **working age** — this may result in the **supply** of workers **decreasing**. Businesses might have to **increase** wages to attract workers, which will result in **increased costs**.

2) **Immigration levels** also impact the **supply** of workers. If lots of **working aged** people are **migrating** into the country, then the supply of workers will **increase**. This can drive **wages down** and **decrease** business **costs**.

Environmental Factors can Increase Business Costs

Nowadays, consumers are **increasingly concerned** with the effect that their purchasing has on the **environment**. This has forced businesses to consider their **impact** on the environment and to do something about it.

1) Businesses pollute the environment through **production** processes, through **traffic pollution** caused by **transporting** raw materials and finished goods, through **dumping waste** in waterways and seas, and through **burying** or **burning waste**. **Packaging** creates a large amount of **landfill** waste and many businesses use up resources in an **unsustainable** way.

2) **Government legislation** forces businesses to deal with some environmental issues (e.g. levels of pollution). Businesses may need to put in place **controls** and **measures** to make sure they are meeting **pollution targets**, which costs the business money. However, if they don't put controls in place and fail to meet government targets, they will incur **large fines**.

3) Some businesses try to **minimise** the **impact** they have on the environment. For example, businesses can try to be more **sustainable** by **replacing resources** as they use them or using **sustainable** or **recycled materials**. A business can adapt its **production process** to make it cleaner, or use renewable energy sources. Product **packaging** is a major issue for retailers — **suppliers** can **adapt** the packaging of their products in order to make them more **appealing** to retailers. E.g. a supplier of tinned vegetables might start to package their products in **cardboard boxes** instead of **metal tins**. However, implementing these things often **increases business costs**.

4) Being **environmentally friendly** can give a company an advantage over competitors and increase **demand**. E.g. Innocent® Drinks strive to be as **sustainable** as possible, which is great for their **public image**. Also, environmental measures can **save** a business money in the long term. **Organisations** have been set up (e.g. Carbon Trust) that aim to help businesses **increase** their **competitiveness** through the changes they make.

Businesses and the External Environment

Ethical businesses have Great Reputations with Consumers

1) **Consumers** are becoming **increasingly concerned** with the ethical and unethical **behaviour** of firms. Not everyone **agrees** on what's ethical and what's not. For example, most people **agree** that **child labour** is **unethical**, but **opinions differ** on whether it's **unethical** to **sell cigarettes** even though they cause cancer.

Ethics are rules which say what is acceptable behaviour for members of a group. Business ethics are about doing the "right thing".

Gus swapped his clothes with a friend. It was not a fair trade.

A sweatshop is a factory (usually overseas) where workers are forced to work long hours in poor conditions for low pay.

2) Some businesses have started to implement **fair trade policies** when **purchasing** from suppliers. This means that the business pays **higher** and **fairer prices** for products (especially those from less-developed countries) with the aim of **improving** the **living standards** of their **supplier's** employees. Obviously this will increase the costs of the business, however it also gives them a **unique selling point** (e.g. The Body Shop® products, The Co-operative's Fairtrade chocolate etc.), which can **increase demand**, allowing them to still be **profitable**.

3) Consumers also care about how a company **treats its workers** — if a company is seen to treat its workers poorly, **demand can drop**. For example, **companies** used to utilise sweatshops to manufacture cheap products, however many have **stopped** following **pressure** (e.g. boycotting) from **customers**.

4) A company that is seen to be **ethical** will have a **great reputation** with customers, so **demand** for the products can be **high** even if they're more **expensive** than rival products. E.g. the shoe company TOMS® gives a lot to children in less-developed countries, so customers don't mind paying extra for the shoes.

Technological Advances can influence Demand and Costs

1) Companies aim to **increase demand** for their products by using **technology** to improve their **marketing**.

2) Many companies now use **technology** to gather **information** about the **lifestyles** of their **customers** and the **products** that they **buy** or are likely to buy (see p.34). This helps them to make sure that **promotions** are **targeting** the right people and stand the best chance of **increasing demand** for products.

3) **Social networking websites** are another way that businesses can use technology to find out more about customer likes and dislikes. People who use these sites often list information about themselves, including the type of **music** they like, where they go on **holiday**, what **car** they drive etc.
Companies can **target** their **advertising** specifically at the people who are **likely** to **buy** their product — this is **cheaper** than advertising to **everyone** and is just as likely to **increase demand**.

4) New technology can also improve **production efficiency**, which can **reduce** business **costs** in the **long-term** (see p.60). However, new technology is **expensive** to set up in the first place. It can also take the jobs of workers, leading to redundancies — this is an **ethical issue** that could impact **negatively** on the **reputation** of the company, which may **affect demand**.

Practice Questions

Q1 What effect would an ageing population have on the demand for products?

Q2 Give two ways in which environmental factors can affect business costs.

Q3 What does it mean for a company to have fair trade policies?

Q4 Write down three effects that ethical behaviour can have on a company.

Exam Question

Q1 A paper company is thinking of pursuing environmental objectives to reduce waste, pollution and deforestation. Analyse the effects this may have on the company in terms of demand for its paper and its costs. [9 marks]

You demand more amazing business know-how? It's gonna cost ya...

You're at the end of the section, but don't stop there. Go back through these pages and make sure you can remember all the different effects that demographics, environmental factors, ethical factors and technology can have on business costs and demand for products. Then you can put your feet up and let everything you've learnt soak in.

Management and Leadership

If you thought management was just telling people what to do, you'd be mistaken — there's a lot more to it than that.

You need to know what **Managers** do

1) Managers **set objectives** for their department, and for the people under them.
   They decide what **work** needs to be done to **meet** the objectives, and what **resources** they need.

2) Managers **analyse** and **interpret data** — e.g. data on employee performance, sales, production costs, etc.

3) Managers **make decisions** — they'll use data analysis and interpretation to do this. For example, if they know that a store is **busiest** between 11 am and 2 pm, they'll **increase** the number of staff during these times.

4) Managers **review** the effectiveness of their decisions, and make **further decisions** based on their **conclusions**. So if a marketing manager had decided to spend more of her budget advertising **one product**, but this had **no impact** on sales, she might decide to spend the money on promoting a **different product** instead.

5) Managers **appraise** their employees' **strengths** and **weaknesses** and **develop** their **talents**.

6) Managers need to be able to **lead** their staff.

> There's a difference between managing and leading. **Managing** means **telling** people what to do and **organising resources** to get the job done. **Leading** means **motivating** people and **inspiring** them to do things. Managers with good leadership skills can **persuade** their staff that their decisions are the **right ones**.

There are different **Management** and **Leadership Styles**

1) **Authoritarian** or **autocratic** style — the **leader** (or **manager**) **makes decisions** on their own. They identify the objectives of the business or department and say **exactly** how they're going to be achieved. It's useful when dealing with lots of **unskilled** workers and in **crisis management**. This method requires lots of **supervision** and monitoring — workers can't make their own decisions. This style can **demotivate** able and intelligent workers.

2) **Paternalistic** (fatherly) style is a softer form of the autocratic style. The leader **consults** the workers before making decisions, then **explains** the decisions to them to **persuade** them that the decisions are in their interest. Paternalistic leaders think that getting **involved** and caring about human relations is a **positive motivator**.

3) **Democratic** style — the leader encourages the workforce to **participate** in the decision-making process. Leaders **discuss** issues with workers, **delegate responsibility** and **listen** to advice. Democratic leaders have to be good communicators. This style shows leaders have a lot of confidence in the workforce — which leads to increased employee **motivation**. It also takes some of the **weight** of decision making off the leader.

4) **Laissez-faire** style is a **weak** form of leadership. **Leaders** might offer employees coaching and support, but they **rarely interfere** in the running of the business. This **hands off** style of leadership would only be appropriate for a small, highly motivated team of **able** workers.

Internal and **External Factors** influence **Management** and **Leadership Styles**

A manager's or leader's **behaviour** is influenced by factors inside and outside the business.
Ideally, they need to **adapt** their style to suit the situation.

Internal Factors

1) **Urgent** tasks need different leadership from **routine** tasks. Urgent tasks, like an **unexpected** large order coming in, may need an **authoritarian** leader to **tell** employees what to do and how to do it.

2) A **large, unskilled** workforce suits **authoritarian** leadership, whereas a **small, educated** workforce suits a **democratic** approach much better.

External Factors

1) In a **recession**, a business needs strong leadership to **guide** it through **difficult economic times**. Authoritarian or **paternalistic** leaders can be efficient in times of crisis — they can issue **clear, quick commands** because they don't have to consult others.

2) When the economy is **growing**, managers don't always need such a strong leadership approach. **Democratic** leaders can take the time to **communicate** with employees.

3) **Increased competition** requires **democratic** leaders who can **motivate** their employees to **adapt** to change or expansion. **Laissez-faire** leaders are more **complacent** and don't always provide enough **leadership** to guide their workforce in this situation.

Management and Leadership

The *Tannenbaum Schmidt Continuum* puts *Leadership Styles* on a *Scale*

The **Tannenbaum Schmidt Continuum** places managers on a scale ranging from **autocratic management** through increasing levels of **participation** in decision-making by the workforce. It identifies **seven key types** of management style.

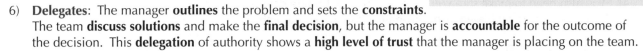

1) **Tells**: **Authoritarian** management style. **Zero involvement** of the workforce in decision making — they're **not** trusted with decisions, so this style can be **divisive** between management and the workforce.

2) **Sells**: The **manager** makes the decision but tries to present it to the workforce as having a **sound rationale**. The workforce are allowed to **ask questions** but they **do not influence** the decision being made.

3) **Suggests**: A decision is **outlined** to the workforce and they are allowed to **discuss** and **ask questions**. This helps them feel that their **opinions** are being **considered**.

4) **Consults**: The manager **proposes** a **tentative decision** and invites **discussion**. The decision is open to being **modified**. This recognizes the **insight** and **value** of workforce participation in decision making.

5) **Joins**: The manager **proposes** a problem and the workforce **work together** to discuss solutions. Ultimately the **manager** will make the **final decision**. This style is useful if the workforce team have **specific knowledge** that helps the manager to make the best decision.

6) **Delegates**: The manager **outlines** the problem and sets the **constraints**. The team **discuss solutions** and make the **final decision**, but the manager is **accountable** for the outcome of the decision. This **delegation** of authority shows a **high level of trust** that the manager is placing on the team.

7) **Abdicates**: The team **define** and **solve** the problem. This is the ultimate level of **freedom** for the workforce . The team are **trusted** to use their **expertise** to make decisions, which should be **highly motivating** for the team. The manager is still **accountable** for the decision, so must be sure the team can handle the **responsibility**.

The *Blake Mouton Grid* lets managers *Assess* their *Leadership Style*

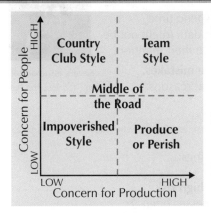

The **Blake Mouton grid** assesses managers based on how much they care about their **employees** and how much they care about **production**.

1) **Impoverished Style**: **Low concern** for **people** and **low concern** for **production**. This is **poor management** of both human and production resources. This results in **low levels of motivation** in the workforce and **low levels of productivity** or **failing quality**.

2) **Produce or Perish Style**: An **authoritarian** focus on the work with strict rules that leads to a **neglect** of workers' **needs** and a **demotivated** workforce. This may result in **high levels** of **absenteeism** and **staff turnover**.

3) **Country Club Style**: An **over-concern** with **worker welfare** and harmony leads to a **happy** but **not very productive** workplace. This leadership style doesn't **motivate** the workers to **increase** their output.

4) **Middle of the Road**: **Average** concern for **worker needs** and **average** focus on **production** leads to **mediocre** results. Although productive output is higher than in the Impoverished or Country Club style, it could be better.

5) **Team Style**: This is seen as the **ideal** leadership style. **High** concern for **people** and **production** creates a **happy**, **motivated** and **productive** workforce. It often uses **non-financial methods of motivation** (see p.93).

Practice Questions

Q1 Give one advantage and one disadvantage of:
       a) a manager who abdicates responsibility for decision-making,
       b) the Produce or Perish style of leadership.

Exam Question

Q1 Analyse the disadvantages of a Blake Mouton 'Middle of the Road' leadership style in a car dealership. [9 marks]

The space time continuum would be much more exciting...

Fun fact: Tannenbaum Schmidt translates as Christmas tree Smith. OK, that probably won't come up in your exams, but the continuum might, so make sure you know all the different leadership styles. Then sing 'O Tannenbaum'.

Management Decision Making

Managers can either make scientific decisions (based on data) or decisions based on intuition.
All decisions come with risks — it's up to the manager to decide whether the risk is worth it.

Decision Making *can be* Scientific...

1) Decisions made **scientifically** are based on **data**, and their **outcomes** are compared to the **initial objectives**. This **model** shows how the scientific decision making process works:

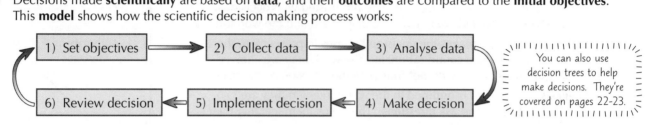

You can also use decision trees to help make decisions. They're covered on pages 22-23.

You can see that this model is a **cycle** — if you **review** your decision and realise that it **isn't working**, you go back to **step 1** and start again.

2) Making decisions based on data **reduces** the risk of making **expensive mistakes**. It is a **logical** and **structured** approach which can be **adapted** if necessary — for example, having analysed the data, you might **review** the objectives, and **change** them if needed.

3) However, it can be **costly** and **time-consuming** because it involves **collecting** and **analysing** a lot of data. It also takes away the '**human element**' so may be **less creative** or **original** than a decision based on intuition.

4) You also need to make sure you have **reliable**, **up-to-date** data. Decisions based on **biased** or **out-of-date** data will be **unreliable**.

... *or* Intuitive

1) **Intuitive** decision making means making decisions based on a **hunch** or **gut instinct**.

2) Some managers have **good intuition** — they can **sense** when a decision is the right one based on **past experience**. When their intuition is right, it can lead to great business decisions and keep the company ahead of its competition.

3) Decisions based on intuition can be made **quickly** — you **don't** have to spend time collecting and analysing data. If the situation is **new** or **unfamiliar**, using data might not be **helpful** (or there might not be any data available), so managers have to use their intuition.

4) It's **risky** to rely on intuition all the time though, because people can make **mistakes**. Decisions made using gut instinct can be **irrational** or not based on logical reasons.

Kevin's intuition told him he'd lost the fight.

Risk, *Reward and* Uncertainty *influence decisions*

When making decisions, managers have to take into account the following things:

RISK All businesses have to take some **risks**. Some decisions can be **high risk**, but if they are successful bring **high rewards** (see below). Businesses often try to **reduce** risk — **scientific decision making** can help with this.

REWARD Managers expect decisions to bring **rewards** (otherwise there'd be no point implementing that decision). Rewards can be **financial** (e.g. **higher sales** or **profits**) or **beneficial** in other ways (e.g. **higher productivity** or **lower staff turnover**).

UNCERTAINTY All business decisions involve some degree of **uncertainty** — no one knows for sure what the outcome of a decision will be. **Scientific decision making** can help **reduce** uncertainty, but you **can't predict** everything, so there will always be some uncertainty.

Managers have to consider all these things when making decisions — for example **borrowing** large amounts of capital in order to **grow quickly** in an **emerging market** could be considered a **high-risk, high-reward** decision. However, if there is a **high** level of **uncertainty**, the manager might decide it's not worth the risk. When there's a lot of uncertainty, managers are **more likely** to make **low-risk, low-reward** decisions — they won't **gain** much, but they won't **lose** much either if it goes wrong.

Management Decision Making

Opportunity Cost is taken into account

1) **Opportunity cost** is the **benefit** that's **given up** in order to do something else
   — it's the **cost** of the choice that's made.

2) It's the idea that **money** or **time** spent doing one thing is likely to mean **missing out** on doing something else.

3) It puts a **value** on the product or business decision in terms of what the business had to **give up** to make it.

4) Businesses must **choose** where to use their **limited resources**. Managers **compare** opportunity costs when making decisions. For example, the opportunity cost of an advert halfway through the X Factor final might be screenings of the same advert in five episodes of Hollyoaks.

5) In more formal terms, opportunity cost is the **value** of the **next best alternative** that's been **given up**.

Managers have to consider Other Factors as well

There are a number of other factors that affect a manager's decision making
— these things have to be taken into consideration too.

> MISSION — A business's **mission** (its **main purpose**) will influence the decisions made. All decisions will take the mission into account.

There's more on mission and objectives on p.3.

> OBJECTIVES — The **objectives** are the medium- to long-term **targets** that help a business achieve its mission. Decisions will be made with the aim of **achieving** the objectives, and are **reviewed** against the objectives to measure their success.

> ETHICS — The firm's **ethics** (moral and social values) have an effect too. E.g. a business might decide **not** to switch to a **cheaper** supplier if that supplier is **less environmentally responsible** than their current one.

> EXTERNAL ENVIRONMENT — The **external environment** is all the **outside factors** that affect a business. It includes things like **competition**, **trends** (e.g. **seasonal** demand and supply), the **economy** of the area or whole country and **environmental** concerns. E.g. if a bakery **lowers** the price of their bread, the marketing manager in a rival bakery might decide to do the same to stay **competitive**.

> RESOURCE CONSTRAINTS — **Resource availability** is also a factor. Resources include **money, people, time** and **raw materials** — a business might not plan to grow if there's a **shortage** of local **labour**, or might not advertise if they don't have much **money**.

Practice Questions

Q1 Describe the six-step model used for scientific decision making.

Q2 Give one advantage and one disadvantage of a) scientific decision making and b) intuitive decision making.

Q3 How might uncertainty affect a manager's decision?

Q4 What is opportunity cost?

Q5 Give three external factors that could influence a decision.

Exam Questions

Q1 Explain one way in which a clothing company's ethical objectives could affect its decision making. [4 marks]

Q2 Which option is a manager most likely to choose when making a decision? [1 mark]
   A high-risk, low reward   B high-risk, high reward   C low-risk, high reward   D low-risk, low reward.

My patience for revision is definitely a limited resource...

Opportunity cost is a bit of a tricky one to get your head around. For example, the opportunity cost of staying up late to watch your favourite TV programme is going to bed early so you're fresh as a daisy in class the next day. You have to decide if the cost of being tired is worth the enjoyment you'd get out of watching the programme.

Decision Trees

Decision trees are a bit like Magic 8-Balls® — they help with decision making.

Decision Tree Analysis combines Probability and Expected Pay-Off

1) When businesses make decisions (e.g. whether to open a new outlet, whether to develop a new product to add to their range), they **know** what the **cost** will be, but often the **outcome isn't certain**.

2) **Probability** is the **likelihood** of an event occurring. Managers often **don't know** how likely it is that an outcome will happen, so they make a **subjective estimate** based on **experience** or **past data**.

3) Probability is usually expressed as a **decimal** in decision trees — e.g. 0.6 for a 60% probability. The probability of an event **happening** and the probability of it **not happening** have to add up to **1** (certainty).

4) The **expected value (EV)** of an outcome is the **probability** of the outcome occurring, **multiplied** by the **pay-off** the business can expect to get. To work out the EV of a **course of action**, you **add** the EVs of the **different outcomes** together.

5) **Net gain** is the financial gain after **initial costs** of the decision have been **subtracted**. Net gain = EV – initial costs.

Learn these Features of Decision Trees

1) A **square** represents a **decision point**. The **lines** coming from a square show the possible **courses of action** and the **costs** of each action.

2) A **circle** shows there are **alternative outcomes** for a course of action, which are shown by **lines** coming out of the circle.

3) The **decimals** on the lines are the **probabilities** of each outcome occurring.

4) The **values in £s** represent the **pay-off** for the business if that outcome happens.

			Outcome 1 0.6 £7 m
	Course of action A (£0.5 m)	Different outcomes	Outcome 2 0.4 £1 m
Decision to be made			Outcome 1 0.8 £10 m
	Course of action B (£2 m)	Different outcomes	Outcome 2 0.2 £2 m
	Do nothing at all		£0 m

Decision Trees show which Course Of Action is probably Best

1) When creating a decision tree, managers first identify which **courses of action** are open to the business.

2) They outline the **possible outcomes** of each course of action and assign **probabilities** to them, estimating the probabilities they don't know.

3) The next step is to **calculate** the **expected value** (EV) and **net gain** of each course of action.

4) Managers should usually choose the course of action with the **highest net gain**.

> **Example — decision tree for launching a new chocolate bar**
>
> A confectionery business is about to launch a new chocolate bar.
>
> 1) With a **marketing** budget of **£15K** the chance of a **successful launch** is estimated at **0.75**. **Without** marketing, the chance is estimated at **0.5**. The basic launch costs are **£1K**.
>
> 2) A **successful** launch would earn a revenue of **£100K** — but if it **failed**, revenue would be **£20K** at best.
>
>
>
> Calculate the **net gain** for each course of action. **Add** the EVs for each outcome together, then **subtract** the initial costs (here, it's the **launch costs**):
>
> <u>With marketing:</u>
> EV = (£100K × 0.75) + (£20K × 0.25) = £75K + £5K = £80K
> **Net gain = £80K – £16K = £64K**
>
> <u>Without marketing:</u>
> EV = (£100K × 0.5) + (£20K × 0.5) = £50K + £10K = £60K
> **Net gain = £60K – £1K = £59K**
>
> Compare the net gain of launching **with** marketing (**£64K**) with the net gain of launching **without** marketing (**£59K**). This shows that spending £15K on marketing is **worthwhile**, so the best course of action is to launch the new chocolate bar after carrying out **marketing**.

Decision Trees

Decision Trees have *Advantages*...

Stay small. The expected benefit from growth is lower than you think.

1) Decision-tree analysis makes managers **work out** and **think about** the **probability** and the **potential pay-off** of each outcome of their chosen action. Managers have to come up with real numerical values for these — much better than vague statements like "this will increase sales".

2) Decision trees are a nice **visual representation** of the potential outcomes of a decision.

3) Decision trees allow managers to compare options **quantitatively** and **objectively**, rather than going for the fashionable option or the option they thought of first.

4) Decision trees are useful in **familiar situations** where the business has enough experience to make **accurate** estimates of **probabilities** and **benefits**.

...and Disadvantages

1) Decision trees are **quantitative** — i.e. they're based on numbers and ignore non-numerical **qualitative data**. **Qualitative data** includes things like the **employees' opinions** about business decisions, and businesses should take qualitative data into account before deciding on a course of action.

2) **Probabilities** are very hard to **predict accurately**. **Estimated pay-offs** are also assumed to be accurate — in real life things may work out differently. If either of these estimates are based on **dodgy** information, the decision is **flawed** too.

3) In reality there's a **wider range** of potential **outcomes** than the decision tree suggests. For example, a new marketing campaign might increase sales for a shorter period than predicted — the decision tree might only allow for success or failure, not for short-term success versus long-term success.

Practice Questions

Q1 Define expected value and net gain and say how each value is calculated.

Q2 Explain the difference between the circles and the squares on a decision tree.

Q3 Outline the stages used in decision tree construction.

Q4 Give one disadvantage of decision-tree analysis.

Exam Question

Q1 Chuse PLC is a multinational business that maintains electronic defence systems. It has won a contract to update the electronics on a submarine. Chuse does not currently have the capacity to complete this contract in the time available. To complete the work in time, Chuse has two options: increase their capacity, or subcontract two-thirds of the work. Expected outcomes are as follows:

Option (cost)	Outcomes	Probability	Profit (£m)
Increase existing capacity (£25 million)	Success	0.6	500
	Failure	0.4	−100
Subcontract (£50 million)	Success	1	300

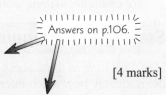

Answers on p.106.

a) On the basis of the information given, construct a decision tree for this problem and label it showing probabilities and forecast pay-offs. [4 marks]

b) Calculate the expected value and net gain for each option. Advise Chuse as to the best option. [8 marks]

c) Analyse the advantages and disadvantages of using a decision tree in this situation. [9 marks]

Decision tree, decision tree, your branches green delight us...

Decision tree analysis is a nifty way for a manager to work out the best option when faced with an important decision. It's based on the potential benefit if things work out well, and the likelihood of it working out well or badly. Work your way through a few decision trees to get the hang of it — don't leave it all until the day of the exam.

Stakeholders and Decision Making

Businesses have to take into account their stakeholders when making decisions. Decisions will affect different stakeholders in different ways — so businesses can try to satisfy all their stakeholders, or just the most important ones.

Businesses have to meet the Needs of Stakeholders

Everyone who is affected by a business is called a **stakeholder**. There are two types: **internal** and **external**.

INTERNAL STAKEHOLDERS — People inside the business

1) The **owners** are the most important stakeholders. They make a profit if the business is successful and decide what happens to the business. In a limited company, the **shareholders** are the owners (see p.12). **Shareholders** usually want high **dividends** and a high **share price**.

2) **Employees** are interested in their **job security** and **promotion** prospects. They also want to earn a **decent wage** and have **pleasant working conditions**. **Managers** have **extra concerns** — they'll probably get some of the blame if the company does badly, and some of the credit if things go well.

EXTERNAL STAKEHOLDERS — People outside the business

1) **Customers** want **high quality** products and services at **low prices**.

2) **Suppliers** are the people and businesses who sell **raw materials** to the business. The business provides them with their **income** — if it can't pay quickly enough, the suppliers can have **cash flow** problems. **Suppliers** want to be paid a **fair price**, and be paid **on time**.

3) The **local community** will **gain** if the business provides **local employment** and **sponsors** local activities. The community will **suffer** if the business causes noise and pollution, or if the business has to **cut jobs**.

4) The **Government** gets more in **taxes** when the business makes good profits.

5) **Creditors** are those who the business owes money to. E.g. a **bank** will want **loans** paid back on time.

Different Stakeholders have Different Objectives

1) Stakeholders all have their own **objectives**, which are often **conflicting**.

2) Businesses have to strike a **balance** to try and keep all their stakeholders as happy as possible. E.g. a business might **cut costs** in order to **increase its profit** if it's trying to keep its **shareholders** happy. But if this reduces the **quality** of the products, **customers** won't be happy and will **stop buying** products — so the plan will backfire.

3) An important balance when making big decisions is between **short-term profit** and **social responsibility**.
   - **Profit** is important — it keeps **different groups** of stakeholders happy. It means **employees** can be **paid well**, **suppliers** have **reliable business**, **shareholders** can expect **dividend payments**, etc.
   - One way to increase profit is to **cut labour costs**. A firm might be able to do this by **relocating** production **abroad**, where labour is cheaper. This decision might satisfy **shareholders** if profit increases, but the **loss of UK jobs** would obviously be **bad news** for **employees** and probably **suppliers** too. The negative impact on the **local community** could damage the **image** of the company with its **customers**.

4) The company must try to satisfy as **many** groups as possible and **still survive financially**. If it can't keep **everyone** happy, the company needs to decide which group to **prioritise** (see below).

5) Stakeholders **don't always disagree** though — sometimes their interests **overlap**. For example, making workers happy can actually help productivity and raise profits.

Stakeholder Mapping considers Power and Interest

Managers have to think about which stakeholder group is most **important** to them. **Stakeholder mapping** helps identify how much **interest** in and **power** (or **influence**) over the business different stakeholders have.

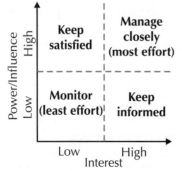

1) A **stakeholder map** helps a business decide how to best **manage** its stakeholders. Each group is mapped to one of four **quadrants**, which determines how much **communication** is needed and how much **attention** is paid to their views when making decisions.

2) Stakeholders with **high levels of power** and **high levels of interest** in the business need to be managed most **closely**, as their satisfaction is **vital** to the business. This group requires the **most effort**.

3) Stakeholders with **little power** and **little interest** in the business require **monitoring** but are **less important** to the business.

Stakeholders and Decision Making

Stakeholder Mapping for a small Italian Restaurant

If you were thinking this whole **stakeholder mapping** thing would make more sense with a **real-life example**, you're in luck. Here's a stakeholder map for a **small Italian restaurant** (i.e. not a chain).

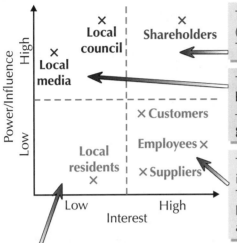

The **shareholders** need to be kept **informed** about new developments (e.g. plans for an outside eating area) and their **opinions** taken into account. They are a **key group** as their investment is **vital** to the restaurant's **future**.

The **local council's environmental health department** has **a lot of power**, but **less** interest in the restaurant. **Local media** can have a **big influence** — if the restaurant is **reviewed** in the local press, it needs to make a **good impression**. These groups mustn't be allowed to become dissatisfied.

The **employees**, **suppliers** and **customers** all have a **strong interest** in the business, but not as much **power** as the **shareholders**. They need to be **informed** about **small changes** and **consulted** on **bigger** ones (e.g. customers should be informed about a new menu and employees should be consulted about changes to opening hours).

Local residents need to be **monitored** to make sure that they are not experiencing any **disturbance** (e.g. from any late night events). This stakeholder group should require the **least communication effort**.

Relationships with Stakeholders are important

1) As well as power and interest, other factors can **influence** a business's **relationships** with its stakeholders. For example, during a **recession**, the business is focusing on **not going bankrupt** so may not be able to fund projects in the **local community**. They may have to **cut wages** and not pay **dividends** as well.

2) Businesses need to **manage** their relationships with stakeholders. If they focus on satisfying **one** stakeholder (e.g. the shareholders) at the **expense** of another (e.g. the employees), it could result in staff **leaving** or **going on strike**, which will **damage** the business. Managing these relationships can **prevent** this from happening.

3) One way of managing relationships is by **consulting** key stakeholders before making any major decisions. Stakeholders are more likely to feel **valued** if their **opinions** are considered. If the stakeholders have **specialist knowledge**, this will benefit the business as well.

4) Good **communication** is vital in managing relationships with stakeholders. For example, keeping **employees** informed about any changes to the business will make them feel included. Businesses can use **social media** and their **website** to communicate with **customers**.

Practice Questions

Q1 Decide whether the following groups are internal or external stakeholders:
   a) part time staff,   b) pressure groups,   c) a bank that loans the business money.
Q2 Give one example where two different stakeholders have conflicting interests.
Q3 Who are the least important stakeholders in the Italian restaurant above?
Q4 Describe one factor that could influence a business's relationship with its suppliers.

Exam Questions

Q1 Construct a stakeholder map for a local leisure centre. You should include at least 4 stakeholders.   [8 marks]

Q2 Analyse the benefits for a high-street fashion chain of using its website and social media to communicate with its stakeholders. You should consider at least 4 stakeholders.   [16 marks]

Employees and vampire slayers — both stakeholders...

Don't get confused between stakeholders and shareholders. Shareholders are stakeholders, but not all stakeholders are shareholders, which is a little befuddling. Anyway, you have to think about how important each group of stakeholders are, and how to keep the most important ones happy (you could write them a poem, that would be nice).

Marketing Objectives

Before a marketing department does anything, it needs to decide what it's aiming for.
Then everyone can work as a team towards the common goal. Much better than random chaos.

Marketing identifies customer Needs and Wants

1) Marketing finds out what customers **need** and **want**. Marketing also tries to **anticipate** what they'll want in the future so that the business can get **one step ahead** of the market.

2) Marketing tries to ensure that the business supplies **goods** and **services** that customers **want** in order to **make a profit**. It's mutually beneficial — the customer gets something they want, the business makes a profit.

3) Marketing covers **research**, **analysis**, **planning** and the "**marketing mix**". The "marketing mix" is all the **decisions** a business makes about promoting and selling a product — see p.40-53.

4) Most larger businesses have a specialised **marketing department** — but marketing affects all departments.

5) Once a company has a **customer base**, marketing helps make sure that customers stay **loyal to that brand** (see p.48 for more on branding).

Marketing Objectives are the Marketing Department's Aims

1) **Marketing objectives** are **targets** that a company's **marketing department** sets itself. They are **valuable** in helping the company to achieve its **overall objectives** (see pages 3-5) and should be **SMART** (see page 4).

2) They tend to **focus** on **sales**, but it's not usually as simple as just "increase sales".
   Marketing objectives are often based on:

Sales Volume and Sales Value

An objective might be to reach a certain **sales volume** (number of units sold) over a certain period of time, e.g. to sell 2 million sewing machines over a year. A sales volume is easy to **visualise**, but it doesn't tell you anything about the amount of money coming in from sales. Businesses that sell a lot of **differently priced** items (e.g. supermarkets) usually base objectives on **sales value** instead, e.g. achieve £500 million in sales over a year.

Sales Growth

A business might aim for a **growth** in sales of a certain **volume** or a certain **value** over a year, e.g. to sell 50 000 **more** sewing machines, or to increase their sales revenue by £50 000 compared to the previous period. Alternatively, they might aim for a certain **percentage growth** in sales, e.g. a 15% increase in the number of sewing machines sold.

Formulas for sales growth, market share and market growth are given on page 28.

Market Share — the percentage of sales in a market made by one firm or brand

A common marketing objective for a business is to **increase their market share** by a certain amount, say 10%. It's useful because it tells a business how well it's doing **compared to its competitors**. To increase market share a business needs to either **entice customers** away from competitors, or **attract brand new customers** in a growing market.

Market Size and Market Growth

The **market size** is the **total number of sales** (or **total value** of sales revenue) in the market over a **period of time**. If the market size increases from one period of time to another (e.g. from one year to the next) then the market is **growing**. A company might set objectives to **stimulate market growth** — as long as the company's **market share** stays the same or grows, they will see an **increase in sales**.

3) The marketing objectives above are **quantitative** — there are **specific figures** to aim for.
   Marketing objectives usually take **more than one** of these figures into account.
   For example, a sales growth target will be decided after looking at the market size and growth
   — a sales target of £2 million is unrealistic if the market size is only £1.5 million.

4) Marketing objectives can also be **qualitative** (**non-numeric**). E.g. improving product **quality**, making sure a particular product **survives** when a rival product enters the market, and creating and maintaining **brand loyalty**.

Brand Loyalty

A business might try to improve its **brand loyalty**, i.e. holding on to **existing customers**, rather than just attracting new ones. **Social media** is a good way of doing this, as it allows **customers** and **businesses** to **interact**.

Marketing Objectives

Marketing Objectives are Influenced by Internal and External Factors

INTERNAL FACTORS

CORPORATE OBJECTIVES — The marketing department has to make sure its objectives are aligned with the company's **overall goals**. For example, if the business wants to **increase profits** in the **short term**, there's no point in the marketing department focusing on a **new product** that's still **two years** away from being **launched**.

FINANCE — The finance department allocates the marketing department's **budget**. This affects what the marketing department is able to do. If the budget is **cut** then marketing objectives may need to be **scaled down**.

HUMAN RESOURCES — **HR planning** (p.88-89) identifies how many **staff** the company needs. If the business has decided to **reduce/increase** staffing levels, marketing will have to adjust its objectives to match what is achievable with these staff levels. E.g. if there are fewer operations staff, the **capacity** (see p.56) will **decrease** so there will be a **limit** to how much marketing can increase **sales volume**.

EXTERNAL FACTORS

MARKET — The **state** of the **economy** has a big impact on marketing objectives. An economic **boom** is a good time to try to increase **sales volumes** since **income levels** are generally higher. In a **recession**, the marketing department is more likely to set an objective of maintaining **market share**.

TECHNOLOGY — In markets where technology changes **rapidly**, marketing objectives tend to be focused on **sales** and **price**, because new technology causes prices to rise or fall very fast. E.g. the price of **regular TVs** has **fallen** rapidly since the introduction of **smart TVs**. Regular TVs might still have a **high market share** because they're so **cheap** — however, it does mean that the marketing department of a regular TV manufacturer will have to **reassess sales objectives** and **pricing strategies** to ensure that they aren't left with **unsold stocks**.

COMPETITORS — The actions of competitors affect marketing objectives, particularly in a highly **competitive** market. If a competitor is focused on **low prices**, then the marketing department may alter their objectives so customers see them as **price competitive**. For example, Microsoft® dropped the price of the Xbox One™ soon after it launched in order to compete on price with the cheaper PlayStation®4.

ETHICS AND ENVIRONMENTAL FACTORS — Ethical and environmental awareness is **increasing** amongst consumers, and behaving in a harmful way can damage a company's **brand image**. For example, some people disapprove of companies that use an **unnecessary amount of packaging**. So a business might change their marketing objectives to include communicating how **ethically and environmentally conscious** they are.

The Law directly affects the Marketing Objectives

Government regulations have a direct impact on the objectives of the marketing department:

- **Predatory pricing** (cutting prices to force a competitor out of business) is illegal in the EU and in the US.
- The **Trade Descriptions Act** regulates promotion. Businesses can't lie about their products.
- Advertising of some products is **restricted**. **Prescription medicines** can't be advertised to the public at all and there are very few places where **tobacco** products can be advertised. Advertising of **alcoholic drinks** is also restricted.

Practice Questions

Q1 Give four quantitative measures that marketing objectives can be based on.

Q2 What is brand loyalty?

Q3 Name two internal and two external factors that influence marketing objectives.

Exam Questions

Q1 If new technology is developed that allows toasters to instantly toast bread, analyse the effects on the marketing objectives of a regular toaster manufacturer. [9 marks]

Q2 Jo Porter has just opened a pub in her local village. Analyse the external and internal influences on the marketing objectives she sets. [9 marks]

No, brand loyalty isn't just for fans of a certain comedian...

Marketing objectives aren't just made up — they're based on market research and marketing data for the product in question. Market analysis and research are covered on the next few pages, then interpreting marketing data on p.32-5.

Market Analysis

A market is just a place where people buy and sell things (whether virtually or physically).
There are different markets for different products (e.g. the electronics market, the cosmetics market, etc.).
Businesses try to get ahead of their competitors by analysing the markets that affect them.

Businesses need to Understand their Market

1) Before a company can try to **sell their product**, they need to **understand** the market they're **operating in**.

2) They need to work out if they're working in a **local**, **national** or **international** market,
whether they're selling things **online** or **physically**, and who their **target audience** is.

3) There are **different ways** that a market can be **classified**:

> - **Geography** (local, national, international)
> - **Nature** of the product (e.g. agricultural, technological)
> - **Seasonality** (seasonal or year-round)
> - **Development** level (new, growing, saturated)
> - Product **destination** (trade, private consumers)

4) Once they've identified their market, the marketing department
can carry out **market analysis** — looking at **sales growth**, **market growth**,
market share and **market mapping**. They can use this analysis to decide
how to market their products.

Firms that sell to other companies are called "business-to-business" (B2B). Ones that sell to consumers are called "business-to-consumer" (B2C).

Market Analysis gives firms information about Market Size and Growth

1) Businesses need to know if the market is **growing** (demand is increasing)
or **shrinking** (demand is decreasing). The formula for **market growth** is:

$$\text{Market growth (\%)} = \frac{\text{New market size} - \text{old market size}}{\text{Old market size}} \times 100$$

If market growth is negative then the market is shrinking.

2) In a **growing** market, **several** firms can **grow easily**. In a **shrinking** market, **competition** can be **heavy** — there
are fewer customers to go around. Firms can **diversify** or they may want to **get out** of the market altogether.

Market Analysis tells firms about their Market Share

1) Market share is the **percentage** of sales in a market
that is made by **one firm**, or by **one brand**.
It's calculated using this **formula**:

$$\text{Market share (\%)} = \frac{\text{Sales}}{\text{Total market size}} \times 100$$

2) E.g. if **40 000** PCs were sold in a given period and **10 000** were made by Dell,
this would give Dell a 10 000 ÷ 40 000 × 100 = **25% market share** (in terms of volume).
If **£5m** was spent on fast-food and **£1m** of this was at KFC®,
this would give KFC® a 1m ÷ 5m × 100 = **20% market share** (in terms of value).

3) It's important to look at **trends in market share** as well as trends in sales revenue. Letting your
market share go down is not good — it means that **competitors** are **gaining an advantage** over you.

Sales Growth can be used to Analyse Market Trends

1) The marketing department will **continuously monitor** the company's **sales growth**
in certain markets to see where it is **gaining sales** and where it is **losing sales**.
The **percentage change** in sales is calculated using the following formula:

$$\text{Sales growth (\%)} = \frac{\text{Sales this year} - \text{Sales last year}}{\text{Sales last year}} \times 100$$

Sales growth doesn't have to be yearly — it can be measured over any time period.

2) If sales growth is **positive** then the company is **gaining sales**,
if sales growth is **negative** then the company is **losing sales**.

3) The marketing department **combines** its analysis of these **figures** in order to see if they are meeting objectives.

> **Example**   A software company reporting an annual increase of **5%** in their game **sales** might seem like
> a good thing. However if the computer game **market** has **grown** by **15%** in the same year then
> they're failing to grow at the **same rate** as the market, so their **market share** has gone down.

Market Analysis

Market Mapping compares Two Features of products or brands

1) A market map shows **extremes** for **two measures** that are important to customers, e.g. low price vs. high price, low quality vs. high quality, basic vs. luxurious, young customer appeal vs. mature customer appeal.

2) It's laid out as a **matrix**, and the products or brands are **positioned** on it according to where they are judged to lie between each pair of extremes.

3) This market map shows how customers ranked 8 **supermarkets**, labelled A to H, in terms of **price** and **quality**.

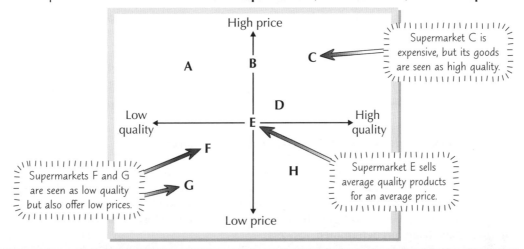

Businesses can get lots of information from Analysing Market Maps

1) Market maps can help a business spot a **gap in the market**. It can try to fill it with a new product or brand, knowing that there won't be any close competitors. Other **market research** will be needed to find out if there is actually **demand** for a product in that gap. E.g. is there a market for high-quality shirts for children?

2) Market maps can show a business who its **closest competitors** are. They can then plan the best **marketing strategy** to persuade customers away from them.

3) If the sales of a product are **declining**, the company might use a **market map** to find out how customers view their product and then try to **reposition** it on the map. Market maps can show the features provided by the most popular brands, which can indicate the **benefits** considered most desirable by the target market.

4) Market maps can show how much customers expect to **pay**, e.g. for cameras of varying quality. This can help a company with its **pricing strategy**.

5) However, market mapping can **simplify** things too much. E.g. in the map above, supermarket A manages to successfully sell **lower quality** goods for **high prices** — this could be due to its **location**, e.g. if it is **conveniently** located within walking distance it means you don't have to drive or use public transport.

6) The positions of products and brands on a market map is usually a **matter of opinion**, and may be **biased**. For example, different people might have **different views** on whether a product is high or low quality.

Practice Questions

Q1 What are the formulas for working out market growth, market share and sales growth?

Q2 What is meant by 'market share'?

Q3 Give an advantage and a disadvantage of market mapping.

Answer on p.106.

Exam Questions

Q1 Henry's Dresses set a 2014 objective to 'increase sales by 10%'. Its sales for 2013 and 2014 are shown in the table on the right.
  a) Determine whether it has met its sales objective.
  b) Evaluate whether the business has performed well.

Year	Sales	Market size
2013	250 units	600 units
2014	290 units	900 units

[2 marks]
[9 marks]

Q2 A manufacturer is planning to launch a new range of cupcakes. Analyse how the manufacturer might use a market map in marketing decision making. [9 marks]

I wish market analysis involved actually going to the market...

Market analysis involves handling data and looking at lots of numbers in order to set the correct objectives and make the right decisions for the company. Make sure you can interpret market maps too and you won't get lost in your exam.

Market Research

Market research is the collection and analysis of market information such as customer likes and dislikes. It's especially important before launching a new product — it helps prevent disastrous errors.

Market Research is done for Three Main Reasons

1) It helps businesses **spot opportunities** — businesses research **customer buying patterns** to aid them in predicting what people will be buying in the future. A business might use **research** to help them spot **growing markets** to get into, and **declining markets** to get out of.

2) It helps them decide **what to do next** — businesses can do some market research before **launching a product** or an **advertising campaign**.

3) It helps them see if their **plans are working**. A business that keeps a keen eye on **sales figures** will notice if their marketing strategy is having the **right effect**.

4) However, market research can be **expensive** and **bad market research** can lead to **disastrous business decisions**. So businesses need to **plan carefully** to make sure they get the **maximum benefit** from market research.

Market Research can be Quantitative or Qualitative

1) Quantitative research produces **numerical statistics** — facts and figures. It often uses multiple-choice **questionnaires** that ask questions like: "When did you last buy this product? A: within the last day, B: within the last week, C: within the last month, D: within the last year, E: longer ago, F: have never bought this product." These are called **closed questions** because they have **fixed**, **predetermined** answers.

2) Qualitative research looks into the **feelings** and **motivations** of consumers. It uses **focus groups** that have in-depth discussions on a product, and asks questions like: "How does this product make you feel?" These are called **open questions**. The answer isn't restricted to multiple-choice options.

Closed questions make analysis easier, but sometimes open questions give more informative data.

Market Research can be Primary or Secondary

Primary market research is where a business **gathers new data** (or employs someone to do it on their behalf). **Secondary market research** is done by **analysing data** that's already available.

Primary Research

1) Primary data is gathered with things like **questionnaires**, **interviews**, post / phone / internet **surveys** and **focus groups** (e.g. a group of well-informed people).

2) Businesses do **test marketing** — e.g. they launch a product in one **region** and measure **sales** and **customer response** before launching it across the country.

3) Primary research uses **sampling** to make predictions about the **whole market** based on a sample (see p.31).

4) Primary data is needed to find out what consumers think of a **new product** or **advert**. You can't use secondary data because, erm, there won't be any secondary data on a brand new product.

5) Primary data is **specific** to the purpose it's needed for. This is great for **niche markets** (see p.39) — secondary data might be too broad or too mainstream to tell you anything useful.

6) Primary data is **exclusive** to the business who researched it, so **competitors can't benefit** from it.

7) However, primary research is **labour-intensive**, **expensive** and **slow**.

Secondary Research

1) **Internal sources** of secondary data include information from loyalty cards, feedback from company salesmen and analysis of company sales reports, financial accounts, and stock records.

2) **External sources** include Government publications like the Social Trends report, marketing agency reports, pressure groups and trade magazines.

3) **Secondary data** is much **easier**, **faster** and **cheaper** to get hold of than primary data.

4) However, secondary data that was gathered for a different purpose might be **unsuitable**. It may contain **errors** and it may be **out of date**.

5) Secondary data is often used to get an **initial understanding** of a market. A business may then do more specific primary research to investigate any **issues** or problems that are shown up by the secondary data.

Market Research

Market Researchers need a Representative Sample

1) Market researchers survey **samples** of people rather than the **whole market** — this is valuable as it keeps their **costs down** and saves them a lot of **time** and **resources**.

2) The sample should try to **represent** the market. It must have **similar proportions** of people in terms of things like age, income, class, ethnicity and gender. If the sample isn't representative, you've got **problems**. However, it isn't always easy to get a representative sample.

3) A **big sample** has a better **chance** of being representative than a **small sample** — but even a big sample won't necessarily be 100% representative. There's always a **margin of error**.

4) The **size** of the **sample** may depend on how many people a company can **afford** to ask. If the **cash** available for research is **limited**, the **risk** of the information being **inaccurate** increases.

5) The **size** of the **sample** and the **sampling method** is also affected by the **type** of product or business, the **risk** involved and the **target market**. E.g. a company producing wedding dresses won't use random sampling (see below) as men don't form part of their target market. They're more likely to use quota sampling instead.

> There are **three** main types of sample:
> - **Simple Random Sample** — Names are picked **randomly** from a list (usually from the electoral register).
> - **Stratified Sample** — The population is divided into groups and people are selected randomly from each group. The number of people picked from each group is **proportional** to the size of the group.
> - **Quota Sample** — People are picked who fit into a **category** (e.g. mums between 30 and 40). Businesses use quota sampling to get opinions from the people the product is directly targeted at.

Market Research needs to Avoid Bias

The **quality** of decisions made using market research is only as good as the **accuracy** of the research.

1) Researchers have to be careful to avoid any possible **bias**.

2) Questionnaires and interviews should avoid **leading questions** — questions that are phrased in a way that **leads** the respondent to give a particular answer, e.g "You do like chocolate, don't you?"

3) Interviews suffer from "**interviewer effects**". This is when the **response** isn't what the interviewee **really thinks**. This can be caused by the **personality** of the interviewer — their **opinions** can **influence** the interviewee.

4) The more **representative** a sample is, the more **confidence** a business can have in the results of the research.

Not Spending enough on market research increases the Risk

1) **Market research** can be very expensive, but not doing enough market research before starting a business **increases the risk** that it will **fail** — businesses don't stand much chance of getting the product right if they **don't know** whether it's really what the market **wants**.

2) It's much less risky to do market research **before** finalising the details of a product. Research may tell a firm that they have to seriously **adapt** and **develop** their original idea to make it **fit in** with what the market **needs**.

Practice Questions

Q1 Give three reasons why firms carry out market research.

Q2 A toy company is researching the market for a new board game. Write three open and three closed questions that they could use in a consumer survey.

Q3 List two internal and two external sources of secondary data.

Q4 What are the three main types of sample, and what are the differences between them?

Exam Question

Q1 Discuss why a new business might pay a market research company to gather primary research for them. [6 marks]

Surveys show that most people lie in surveys...

Research takes time and costs money — businesses must make sure the data's accurate or it'll be as much use as a chocolate fireguard. They also have to actually use the findings to provide what their customers want. If a business can use market research to increase their sales and profits, the market research will pay for itself. Everyone's a winner.

Interpreting Marketing Data

Businesses have a lot of mathsy techniques for analysing data, and you need to know how they work.

Time Series Analysis looks at data over Time

1) **Time series analysis** is used to reveal **underlying patterns** by recording and plotting data over time. For example, the recording of **sales** over a year.

2) **Trends** are the long-term movement of a variable, for example the sales of a particular product over a number of years. Trends may be **upward**, **constant** or **downward**, but there are usually **fluctuations** around the trend.

3) **Seasonal** fluctuations repeat on a **regular** basis — such as daily, quarterly or yearly, e.g. the use of electricity over a 24-hour period, or the sales of ice lollies over a year.

4) **Random** fluctuations have **no pattern** to them. They also include the results of **major disturbances** like **war**, changes of **government, natural disasters** and sudden **unpredictable events,** e.g. the 2013 "horse meat" scandal.

5) Time series analysis can also be used to look for **links** between **sales** and **marketing** activity. For example, the marketing department might look at trends in sales to see if their **marketing campaigns** are working, and make **decisions** about future campaigns based on these **trends**.

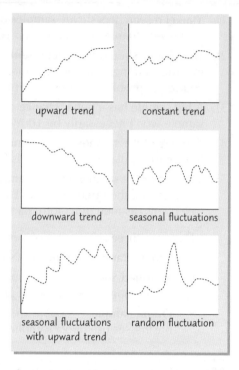

upward trend   constant trend

downward trend   seasonal fluctuations

seasonal fluctuations with upward trend   random fluctuation

Extrapolation can be used to Predict Future Sales

1) **Trends** in sales data from previous years can be continued into the future (**extrapolated**) to **forecast future sales**. This allows managers to set **sales targets**. Sales **performance** can be measured against these targets.

2) For example, if sales have increased by **8% a year** for the past five years, extrapolation will predict that they'll **continue** to do so in future years.

3) In reality, increases or decreases **won't be the same** every year — marketing can use the **average** increase or decrease over a **few years** to extrapolate into the future:

- The revenue for this business increased by **£40 000** between 2010 and 2014 (**4 years**) — that's an **average** of **£10 000 a year** (40 000 ÷ 4). This average can be used in extrapolation.

- So in **2017** you might predict that the revenue will be **£310 000**. In order to achieve this target, marketing might set the objective of increasing sales by **3.5%** each year for the next **3 years**.

- However, this prediction **doesn't** take into account that the rate of growth was **slowing down** between 2010 and 2013 (the increase in growth between 2013 and 2014 could have been a **random fluctuation**). It also doesn't factor in other influences like **market share** or **market growth**.

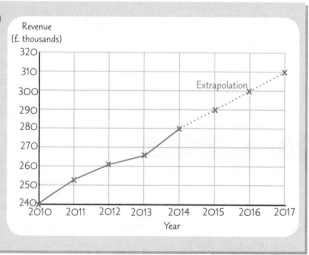

4) Extrapolation is most useful in fairly **stable** environments, e.g. where the **size** of the **market** or the number of **competitors** is **unlikely** to **change** much.

5) Extrapolation relies on **past trends** remaining **true**. Unfortunately, the **pace of change** in the market can be very fast, so extrapolations from the past don't always predict the future very accurately — it's best to use it for predicting just a **few months** ahead because customer desires and technology constantly change.

6) **Sudden unexpected events** are the biggest pitfall for extrapolation. Changes in the market due to things like **new technology** make extrapolation from past data completely useless.

Interpreting Marketing Data

Correlation shows how Closely two Variables are Related

1) **Correlation** is a measure of how **closely** two variables are **related** — for example, the age of customers and their income. Correlation may be **positive** or **negative**, **strong** or **weak**, or there may be no apparent correlation at all.

2) You can draw a **line of best fit** through a set of correlated points — the line should be as **close** as possible to **all** the **points** on the graph.

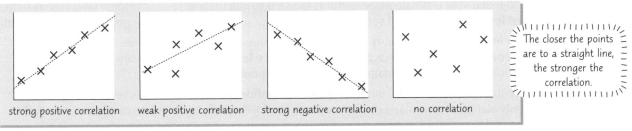

strong positive correlation   weak positive correlation   strong negative correlation   no correlation

The closer the points are to a straight line, the stronger the correlation.

3) It's a **useful tool**, but correlation **doesn't** prove **cause and effect**. **Other variables** may be important — e.g. there might be a **strong positive correlation** between ice cream sales and sun cream sales, but one does not **cause** the other. They're both **affected** by an **external factor** — e.g. the weather.

4) **External factors** have to be taken into account when **reviewing correlation**. For example, if sales of sports equipment increased during a **marketing campaign** then you might say sales increased because of the marketing campaign. However, if the marketing campaign happened to **coincide** with the Olympic Games then it's not clear whether marketing or the event had a **bigger impact** on sales.

5) If there's a **correlation** between two variables, managers might assume that the trend will **carry on**. They can **extrapolate** the graph — draw a **line of best fit** and then keep the line going to **project** the trend **further** along the **horizontal axis**. For example, if the graph shows the **cost of car repairs** against the number of **miles driven**, the line can be **extrapolated** to **predict** the cost of repairs after **any** number of miles. However, they need to be cautious about extrapolating too far beyond the known data as the trend might not continue.

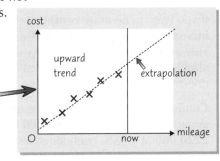

Sales Forecasts can help Other Departments

1) Sales forecasts allow the **finance** department to produce **cash flow** forecasts — they can use **predicted sales** to work out how much money is expected to **come in** and how much they have to **spend**. (See page 73 for more on cash flow forecasting.)

2) Sales forecasts also allow **production** and **human resources** departments to prepare for the expected level of sales. They can make sure that they have the right amount of machinery, stock and staff. (See page 88 for more on HR planning.)

Practice Questions

Q1 What is a trend?

Q2 What is extrapolation? How can a business use extrapolation?

Q3 What is correlation?

Answer on p.106.

Exam Question

Q1 The graph on the right shows the sales figures for a children's computer tablet.
   a) By drawing and extrapolating a line of best fit on the graph, estimate the revenue in 2015. **[3 marks]**
   b) Do you think this estimate is likely to be accurate? Justify your answer. **[16 marks]**

A little less extrapolation, a little more action please...

Extrapolation is all about identifying a trend and then predicting what will happen next. It's important for businesses to look at past performance because it will give them an idea of how a product will sell in the future. But don't forget, it's not 100% reliable — sudden events can really throw a spanner in the works and mess up your marketing strategy.

Interpreting Marketing Data

A bit of statisticky stuff first and then some ways that technology is used to find out about you and your interests.

Confidence Intervals are a Margin of Error for sample results

1) No matter how carefully you select your sample there's a good chance that it **won't** represent the **whole population** accurately. Any result taken from the sample will just be an **estimate** of the equivalent value for the **population**.

> The population is the whole group that you want to find out about. E.g. all a business's customers.

2) One way to make your estimate more useful is to use it to calculate a **confidence interval** — a **range of values** that you're fairly sure the value for the population will lie within.

3) **Confidence levels** indicate how **sure** you are that the value for the population lies **within** the **confidence interval** — e.g. a **95% confidence level** means that you are 95% certain that your confidence interval contains the value for the population.

4) You choose the **confidence level**, then **calculate** the **confidence interval** for this level using a nasty statistical formula. Luckily you don't have to be able to calculate confidence intervals, just understand how they're used.

> **Example:** A cleaning company sets an objective of **80% customer satisfaction**. They ask a sample of their customers and find that **84%** of them are satisfied. Using this estimate and a **confidence level** of **95%**, they calculate a **confidence interval** of **82%** to **86%** customer satisfaction.
>
> This means that they are **95% confident** that the percentage of satisfied customers lies between 82% and 86%. So they can be fairly sure that **more than 80%** are satisfied, which means that they've **met their objective**.

5) If you want to be **more confident** that your interval contains the **value** for the **population**, you can **increase** the **confidence level**. This will give you a **wider** confidence interval.
However, wide confidence intervals can be too **vague** to be helpful. E.g. for the cleaning company example above, a 99% confidence interval might be calculated as **78%** to **90%** customer satisfaction. This interval doesn't help them to decide if they've met their objective because it includes values **below** their target of 80%.

6) **Confidence intervals** can also be used to show uncertainty in **predicting** other figures — e.g. if the marketing department predicts sales of **£200 000**, they might say that the actual sales will be between **£180 000** and **£220 000** at a **95%** confidence level.

Technology can be used to gather Information about Customers

Many companies now use **technology** to gather **information** about the **lifestyles** of their **customers** and the **products** that they **buy**. This helps them to make sure that **promotions** are **targeting** the right people.

1) Lots of supermarkets offer **loyalty cards** which give customers money back according to how much they spend. The **benefit** for the supermarket is that it not only allows them to form a **database** of customer names and addresses, but also their **preferences** based on what they **buy**. E.g. they could target an offer on pet insurance at people who bought pet food. This would make the campaign **cheaper** and **more effective**.

2) **Social networking websites** are another way that businesses use technology to find out more about their customers.

- Facebook® has tools that **analyse** which other pages a company's **followers** are **interested** in — this allows the company to build a **profile** of its customers for relatively **minimal cost**.

- Facebook® can also be used to find out the **demographics** (see p.16) of people interested in existing products — so if a company wants to **market** a **new product** it can see what kinds of people like **similar products**.

- Companies who **advertise** on social media sites can make their adverts visible only to the people who have shown an interest in **similar products** before — this is **cheaper** and more **effective** than targeting everyone who uses the website.

- Businesses can also use **social media** to follow **what people are saying** about their products and also competitors' products. This is **cheaper** and **more immediate** than organising surveys.

3) **Search engines** like Google™ often use targeted advertising too — they show adverts that are **relevant** to the topic the user searched for.

4) Controversially, some stores use **Wi-Fi®** signals from customers' **phones** to track their movements — they can then use this data to help them plan the **best store layout**. For example, they can identify the areas of the store that **most customers** walk past and display their **best promotions** and **offers** there.

Interpreting Marketing Data

IT can be used to help Analyse Marketing Data

Most companies use **software** to do their marketing analysis. The **advantages** of this are:

1) Computers can process much **more data** than people can. Computer software can analyse huge amounts of data and produce sales forecasts more quickly than people can. Using computers can also **reduce** the risk of **errors**.

2) There are many types of market analysis software, so a business can find a program that fits its **needs** exactly. For example, marketing analysis software allows managers to investigate "**what if?**" scenarios. They can work out the impact of **potential changes** in expenditure or sales, which helps them to plan their marketing decisions.

3) IT can also be used to analyse data gathered at the **point-of-sale**. As soon as an item has been sold, it is recorded — so the effect of vouchers/coupons and marketing campaigns can be seen immediately.

4) '**Big data**' is a new term used to describe the **vast quantities** of data from all sources, e.g. data with a structure such as sales and customer information, and unstructured data such as that from social networking. The trouble is there is so much data and it streams in so fast that normal computers aren't sufficient to handle it. Large companies are investing in ways of **analysing big data** to draw **useful correlations**.

5) There are **downsides** to analysing marketing data using IT:

   - Buying **software** can be **expensive**. If a new version of the software is released and the business decides to **upgrade**, it costs even more money.

   - Staff need to be **trained** to use the software, which might be **expensive** and **time-consuming**. If the company **upgrades** their software at any point, further training might be needed.

   - There's a risk that having software that can deal with loads of data will lead to the company valuing the **quantity** of information over its **quality**. A business might produce lots of pretty graphs, but if nobody's drawing **conclusions** about what the **trends** mean for the company they're not useful at all.

   - Companies with lots of data might find that their **computer systems** aren't up to the job of **handling** it, e.g. if it takes too long to upload all the information. If this happens, they might have to **outsource** (see p.65) their marketing analysis to a **specialist company** or stick to analysing just a **proportion** of the available data.

Example

Problem: When Tesco launched its **loyalty card**, Clubcard, in 1995, it took **30 hours** every time they **transferred the data** they'd collected from their computers to the computers of the **data analysis** firm that interpreted it.

Solution: Tesco decided that it would be easier to **interpret** just **some of the data** and then apply their findings to the **rest of the data**. They agreed that the **data analysis** firm dunnhumby would look at 10% of the data once a week and **extrapolate** their findings to the other 90% of Clubcard holders. Dunnhumby have since introduced **new software** which allows them to analyse the behaviour of **all** Clubcard holders without relying on extrapolation.

Practice Questions

Q1 Why are confidence intervals used when reporting market research data?

Q2 Give three ways that technology can be used to gather information about customers.

Q3 Give two advantages and two disadvantages of using IT to analyse data.

Exam Question

Q1 Using sample data, a business estimates the average age of their customers and calculates a 99% confidence interval for this age. The interval extends from 44 to 60. Which of the following is most likely to be the true average age of their customers?

A 42   B 50   C 61   D 69   [1 mark]

Confidence interval — a short break for a little pep talk...

Increasing the confidence level means you're more sure of your results, but that the interval will be less precise and probably less useful. E.g. it's not very helpful to claim that, at the 99.9% confidence level, between 10% and 90% of the population would buy the new product.

Interpreting Elasticity of Demand

OK, so price isn't the only thing that affects demand, but it can certainly have a pretty major impact...

Price Elasticity of Demand shows how Demand changes with Price

1) The **price elasticity** of a product is how much the price change **affects** the demand. It is found using this **formula:**

$$\text{Price elasticity of demand} = \frac{\%\text{ change in quantity demanded}}{\%\text{ change in price}}$$

2) Price elasticity of demand is **always negative** (a positive change in price causes a negative change in demand, and a negative change in price causes a positive change in demand) so you can just **ignore** the **minus sign**.

3) If the price elasticity of demand is **greater than 1** (ignoring the minus sign), the product is **price elastic**. If the price elasticity of demand is **less than 1**, it's **price inelastic**. So, –1.5 is price elastic and –0.5 is price inelastic.

Example: A price **rise** of **10%** results in a **30% reduction** in demand.

As price goes up, demand falls — and vice versa.

$$\text{Price elasticity of demand} = \frac{-30\%}{+10\%} = -3 \text{ so this product is } \textbf{price elastic.}$$

You won't have to work out elasticity coefficients in your exam — just use and interpret them.

Example: A price **reduction** of **20%** results in a **5% increase** in demand.

$$\text{Price elasticity of demand} = \frac{+5\%}{-20\%} = -0.25 \text{ so this product is } \textbf{price inelastic.}$$

This is called the elasticity coefficient.

4) For **price elastic** products, the **% change in demand** is **greater than** the **% change in price**.

5) For **price inelastic** products, the **% change in demand** is **less than** the **% change in price**.

Price Elasticity affects Revenue and Profit

1) **Sales revenue = price of product × quantity sold** (see p.6). Price elasticity shows how price affects sales revenue.

2) If a product is **price elastic**, a **price increase** will make **sales revenue go down**. The money lost from the **% decrease in sales** will be **more than** the money gained from the **% increase in price**.

Example: 100 scarves a year are sold for **£10 each** giving a revenue of **£1000**. Price elasticity coefficient = **–2.5**. If the company **increases** the price by **10%** to **£11**, demand will **decrease** by 10% × 2.5 = **25%**. So 75 scarves will be sold at the new price, which **decreases revenue** to 75 × £11 = **£825**.

3) For **price elastic products**, a firm can **increase revenue** by reducing price, as it increases the number of sales.

4) If a product is price **inelastic**, a rise in **price** will make **sales revenue go up**. The money lost from the **% decrease in sales** will be **less than** the money gained from the **% increase in price**.

Example: If the scarves' price elasticity coefficient is **–0.5** and price **increases** by **10%**, demand will **decrease** by 10% × 0.5 = **5%**. So 95 scarves will be sold at the new price, which **increases revenue** to 95 × £11 = **£1045**.

5) For **price inelastic products**, **decreasing** the **price** will make **sales increase** slightly, but sales **revenue goes down** because the price has fallen and only a few more units have been sold.

Price Elasticity of Demand Depends on Ease of Switching

1) **Necessary products** like milk are **price inelastic**. Changing the prices doesn't have much affect on demand. If consumers can **switch** to **similar** or **competitor** products, demand will be **price elastic**. E.g. if Princes tuna increases in price, people might buy John West tuna instead.

iPhones® are price inelastic due to the strength of the Apple® brand.

2) Businesses try to **differentiate** their products to create **brand loyalty**. **Loyal** customers won't switch even if the price goes up, so this makes the product **less** price elastic.

3) Price elasticity of demand increases over time as customers have chance to find alternative products. The **internet** makes it easy to find alternatives and so **increases price elasticity**.

4) **Product types** tend to be **price inelastic**, but individual **brands** tend to be **price elastic**.

Petrol sales are inelastic but sales of an individual company's petrol are elastic.

5) Items costing a **greater proportion** of consumers' incomes will be more **price elastic**. Customers won't be too concerned about a 10% rise in the cost of a newspaper, but a 10% increase in the price of a car might cause them to look for **alternatives**.

Interpreting Elasticity of Demand

Income Elasticity of Demand shows how Demand changes with Income

When people earn **more money**, there's **more demand** for some products, and **less demand** for other products.

Income elasticity of demand = $\dfrac{\text{\% change in quantity demanded}}{\text{\% change in real income}}$

Example: A rise in income of **10%** results in a **5% increase** in demand.

Income elasticity of demand = $\dfrac{+5\%}{+10\%} = +0.5$

Change in real income means change in income, taking into account how prices have changed (usually increased) over the same period.

1) **Normal goods** (e.g. fresh fruit and vegetables) have a **positive income elasticity of demand** that's **less than 1**. This means that as **income rises**, the **demand rises** — but at a **slower rate** than the increase in income.

2) **Luxury goods** (e.g. designer clothes and fine wines) have a **positive income elasticity of demand** which is **more than 1**. This means that the **demand for luxury goods** grows **faster** than the increase in income.

3) In a business sense, "**inferior**" goods are cheaper 'value' products — e.g. a **cheaper supermarket value brand** of baked beans compared to **Heinz® Baked Beans**. Inferior goods have a **negative income elasticity of demand** — demand falls when **income rises** and **demand rises** when **income falls**.

If demand rises, revenue increases. If demand falls, revenue decreases.

Elasticity helps a business make Choices

1) **Price elasticity** helps a manufacturer **decide** whether to **raise** or **lower** the price of a product. They can see what might happen to the **sales**, and ultimately what will happen to **sales revenue**.

2) **Income elasticity** helps a manufacturer see what will happen to sales if the **economy** grows or shrinks.

3) Here are examples of the **marketing decisions** that might be made about two products:

Tin of value tomato soup — price elasticity of demand = –3.0, income elasticity of demand = –0.5

- **Reduce** the price to **increase demand** and **sales revenue**, but **only** if the profit margin is big enough.
- In times of **economic growth**, sales will **fall** so the **brand image** of the product may need to be changed to appeal to better-off customers. In times of **recession**, demand for the product will **increase**.

New designer kitchen — price elasticity of demand = –0.4, income elasticity of demand = +1.5

- **Increase** the price — demand will **fall slightly**, but revenue and profit will still **increase**.
- In times of **economic growth**, sales will **grow** so the aspirational **brand image** should be maintained. In times of **recession**, demand for the product will **fall**, so **incentives** such as discounts and interest-free repayments over a number of years could be introduced to **encourage sales**.

Practice Questions

Q1 If a product has an elasticity coefficient of –0.9, is it price elastic or inelastic?

Q2 Give three factors that affect price elasticity.

Q3 What kind of products become less popular when there's an increase in income?

Exam Questions

Answer on p.106.

Q1 A company sells 200 horses a year for £1500 each. If the elasticity coefficient is –0.7, calculate the impact on revenue that a 15% increase in prices will have. [7 marks]

Q2 The price elasticity of demand for a pack of sausages is estimated to be –0.2. Explain what this means and analyse the effect changes in price will have on revenue. [9 marks]

Rubber prices are usually the most elastic...

The clues are in the names — price elasticity shows how much price influences demand, and income elasticity shows how much income affects demand. Luckily, you won't be asked to calculate the elasticity coefficients in your exams.

Marketing Decisions — STP

Now it's time to divide and conquer the market. That's what STP is all about.

STP — Segment, Target, Position

STP aims to **focus** marketing efforts where they'll be **most effective**. It is a marketing process with **three stages**:

SEGMENT	**TARGET**	**POSITION**
Divide the market into **groups** with **similar characteristics** or needs, e.g. into age or income groups.	Decide **which** market segment to focus on and adapt the **product** and the **marketing mix** to appeal to this group.	Position the product in the **target customers' minds** so they see it as better than the competition.

There are Different ways to Segment a market

1) Segmentation **divides** a market into **groups** of buyers. Each group will have different wants and needs, and require a **different marketing mix** (see p.40). E.g. they'll differ in how much they're prepared to spend, and where and when they shop. They'll also use different forms of **media** — e.g. TV, magazines, social media platforms.

2) Here are some of the methods or 'bases' used to segment a market:

Demographic	**Age**, e.g. Saga Holidays are aimed specifically at the over-50s.
	Gender, e.g. yoghurts are mainly marketed towards women.
	Socio-economic class, e.g. businesses can segment their market based on the kind of **jobs** people have — e.g. **modern one bedroom flats** might be marketed at **young professionals**.
	Family size, e.g. large **"family packs"** of breakfast cereal, loo roll, etc. are aimed at large families.

Geographic	The market can be divided according to **neighbourhood**, **city**, **county**, **country**, or **world region**, e.g. Asia. It's a method mostly used by **multinational** companies as their customers have a range of cultures, lifestyles and climates and are likely to need **different marketing mixes**. An example closer to home is that the core market for **Irn-Bru** is **Scotland**.

Income	E.g. CHANEL makeup is aimed at customers with **high incomes**, and Tesco's own-brand makeup is aimed at lower-income customers. **Luxury products** are usually aimed at high income groups.

Behaviour	**Amount of use**, e.g. mobile phone suppliers market **differently** to heavy users and light users.
	Lifestyle, e.g. busy **young workers** might tend to buy lots of microwaveable ready-meals, so a company making **ready-meals** might target this market segment.

3) Segmentation is useful for **identifying new customers**, **markets** and **products**. It can also help to identify the **best way** to market a product (e.g. advertising high-end cosmetics in Vogue magazine).

4) However, segmentation can cause companies to **ignore the needs** of **potential customers**. It can be difficult to **break** the market into **obvious segments** and even more difficult to find ways of marketing to **specific demographics**.

Target Big enough segments, with Potential Growth and Little Competition

Once you've segmented the market, you need to decide **which segments** to **target**. There are **three approaches**:

Concentrated marketing involves targeting **one or two segments**. It's a good approach for smaller businesses with **limited resources**. The segment must be **big enough** for a decent return, have **growth potential** (e.g. sports clothing for pensioners). It should also have a **need** that the business can meet (that **isn't** already met by lots of **competitors**).

Differentiated marketing is where **several segments** are targeted, and the product and marketing mix is **adapted** to appeal to **each** segment. This is only really feasible for **large companies** with large budgets. E.g. the same colouring book could be advertised to children as a fun activity, or to adults as a relaxation aid.

Undifferentiated marketing is where the segments are **ignored** and the company tries to reach the **entire market** with a single product and marketing mix. It makes sense for **widely used products**, e.g. toothpaste. It has the advantage of potentially **high sales volumes** and **relatively low marketing costs**.

Marketing Decisions — STP

Businesses can target Niche or Mass Markets

1) Concentrated marketing is also known as **niche marketing**.

2) Focusing on **niche markets** often means small businesses don't have to compete **directly** with larger businesses (who don't normally target niche markets). E.g. a small business selling microwave meals could **establish a niche** by **specialising** in, say, meals for people with nut allergies — this allows the business to make a profit even though there are lots of large ready-meal businesses.

3) A small manufacturer can **meet the demand** of a small niche more easily than it can meet the demand of a **mass market**. It can also be easier to market their product to a niche. E.g. a new type of fishing bait could be promoted in a fishing magazine.

4) Some products are aimed at a **mass market** (often with undifferentiated marketing) — they're designed to appeal to **lots of consumers**, e.g. Coca-Cola®.

Position a product in Customers' Minds

1) Once a company has decided which **segments** it's going to **target**, it needs to think about **positioning**.

2) Positioning is **creating an image** of your brand or product in the **mind** of your **target customer**. It's getting **them** to develop the opinion of your product that **you** want them to.

3) Customers have a **mental map** of the market and will **position** new products relative to the alternatives. So a business needs to look at where would be the most effective place to **position** its brand or product in relation to its **competitors**. E.g. if it can't **compete** with competitors on **price** or **quality** it might push the **convenience** or **ethical nature** of the product.

4) To position your product well, you need to convince the target customers that your product has **benefits** for them and to **differentiate** it from the competition in a way that is **relevant** to them.

> **Example:** An **outdoor clothing** company targeting **young back-packers** might choose to position its range of outdoor clothing as more **ethical** than **rival products** because its market **research** has highlighted **ethical sourcing** as a feature that young back-packers **care about**.

Influences on positioning

- **State of the market** — if the economy is in **recession** then companies will be more likely to **position** their brand or product to make customers think it offers the **best value for money**. Whereas in a booming market they might emphasise that their product is **great quality** or **environmentally-friendly**.

- **Company's current products** — if the company's other products are seen as **reliable** and **cheap** they are likely to try and position any new products in a similar place.

- **Attributes of the company** — companies need to position products to match their **strengths and weaknesses**. E.g. if a business is really **innovative** then it will focus on how its products are **cutting-edge** and **unique**.

Practice Questions

Q1 Outline the STP process.

Q2 Give four bases for segmenting the market.

Q3 Give two things you should consider when picking a segment to target.

Exam Questions

Q1 A small manufacturer is launching a new brand of luxury suntan lotion. Analyse how the STP process could be used in marketing the lotion. [9 marks]

Q2 A new archery equipment store has opened. Analyse the advantages and disadvantages of targeting specific markets over targeting the entire market. [9 marks]

Any customer can have a car painted any colour — so long as it is black...

That's what Henry Ford famously said in 1909 about one of the first mass marketed cars — the Model T. Mr Ford churned them out cheaply and advertised them in mass media. Then along came General Motors, who segmented the market by income and type of car wanted — their aim was to make a car for each segment. Which was a lot of cars.

Marketing Decisions — The Marketing Mix

The marketing mix used to just have 4Ps in it. But lucky for you, some marketing guru thought up an extra 3Ps.

The **Traditional Marketing Mix** — *Product, Price, Place, Promotion*

The marketing mix describes the **factors** that firms consider when **marketing** a product — they're the factors that'll make customers either buy a product or not buy it.

It used to be known as the **4Ps**. The **price** has to be right, the **product** has to be right, the product must be distributed through the right **places**, and it has to be **promoted** in the right way.

The **Extra 3Ps** — *People, Physical Environment, Process*

Cindy thought the 7Ps were
Party, Party, Party, Party,
Party, Party and Penguin.

Service industries supply **people** to **help** or **work** for customers — they have become the **biggest sector** of the UK **economy** and so **3 extra Ps** have been added to the **marketing mix**.
These Ps are particularly **important** for services, but are part of the marketing mix for **physical goods** too.

| People | People are the most important part of a service business. A customer is more likely to buy a service if the people providing it are **well-trained**, **knowledgeable**, **reliable**, **friendly** and **efficient**. |

| Physical Environment | The presentation of the **environment** where a service is delivered is important. E.g. customers expect a hair salon to be **clean** and **stylishly decorated**, with a comfy sofa on which to read magazines as you wait. Grubby seats and peeling wallpaper won't attract many customers. |

| Process | This includes things such as **waiting times**, the **ordering** and **payment systems** and any **after-sales service**. E.g. the option to pay with PayPal might influence whether a customer buys from a particular online company. |

There's more on each of the 7Ps on pages 42-53.

In an **integrated marketing mix** the 7Ps need to **work together** and **complement** each other — if just one of the factors is **wrong**, it can **decrease** the **revenue** generated from the product.

Example: A company develops an innovative new **product**, but has an inefficient ordering and delivery **process**. This means customers have **trouble ordering** the product, and have to **wait** weeks for it to be delivered. The company will get a **bad reputation** among customers and will sell **fewer products**.

Different Factors influence the *Integrated Marketing Mix*

1)   The integrated marketing mix shouldn't be based on guess work — the right **market research** helps companies develop the right mix of the 7Ps, and make the best **marketing decisions** based on these Ps.

2)   **Competitors** in the market can influence the marketing mix — the **price** of a product will be directly influenced by the price of similar products. A high level of competition might mean the company spends more on **promotion** and more **people** are recruited and trained to offer better **customer service** than competitors.

3)   The **target market segment** influences the marketing mix. E.g. wealthy consumers will be **less price sensitive** than low income consumers. Also, certain market segments will see different forms of **media promotion** — e.g. young working people, who could be the target market for a new trendy ready-meal brand, might not see adverts on daytime TV.

4)   Where the company wants to **position** a **product** in the minds of customers will impact all areas of the marketing mix. For example, PANDORA bracelets highlight that their product is high quality by having **well-trained** and **knowledgeable staff** selling **expensive** products in **exclusive**, **stylish stores**.

5)   The **location** of a business will determine what is realistic when it's putting together its marketing mix. E.g. a business that's based in Alaska might not be able to include next-day delivery to the rest of the world as part of its **process**.

6)   The **type of product** you are marketing will affect the importance of each of the 7Ps in the marketing mix. E.g. **promotion** and **physical environment** aren't that important for **cheap** products (e.g. plastic cups) whereas they are very important for **expensive** products (e.g. high-end sports cars).

7)   Whether you're selling **goods** or a **service** will affect the mix, as will whether you're selling to another **business** or to **consumers**.

8)   Other factors to do with the product, such as the **product life cycle** and the business's **product mix** influence the marketing mix. These factors are covered on p.42-45.

Marketing Decisions — The Marketing Mix

The Resources of a Business affect the Marketing Mix

The integrated marketing mix is influenced by factors within the business:

1) The **marketing** and **corporate objectives** of a business will affect the marketing mix — for example, if an airline wants to increase its **brand loyalty** it might offer frequent fliers an exclusive departure lounge, extra customer service and **promotions** on the **prices** of certain tickets.

2) Many businesses have to **compromise** on certain aspects of the marketing mix due to their **finances**. E.g. a small firm might not have enough **money** to promote a niche product through TV adverts, promotional pricing and point-of-sale displays, so they must choose the **most effective** method of promotion that they can afford.

3) Suppliers tend not to offer **credit** or **discounts** to small businesses so they are only able to produce **small quantities** of goods at a time. This will impact the **price** and **process** aspects of the marketing mix.

4) Businesses that don't have the right **software** to monitor customers' details will have to spend extra money on **promoting** products as they **can't** market directly to **repeat customers**.

5) A company with a well-respected, luxurious **brand image** will be able to charge more for their products than a budget brand. In fact, it'd probably be a **bad idea** for them to lower their prices as this might affect their image.

6) The **knowledge and skills of employees** might mean businesses can justify **increasing prices**. E.g. at Halfords, employees will help you find the correct bulb or wiper blade for your car and even fit it (for an extra payment). However, these services need to be **promoted** so people know about them.

Changing the Marketing Mix can help to make a business More Competitive

1) **Markets** are **dynamic** (constantly changing) — new competitors/products are constantly **entering** the market and failed ones are **leaving**. The integrated marketing mix needs to **adapt** to these changes.

2) In order to **remain profitable**, companies need to keep **reviewing** their **marketing mix** and **altering** their marketing decisions, taking into account the actions of **competitors** and **other changes** in the marketplace.

3) For a company to stay profitable, it needs to stay **competitive**. A business is competitive if it has something that **customers want** or **need** that **other** similar **businesses don't** have.

- A company can **improve** its **competitiveness** by **changing** any one of the seven elements in the **marketing mix**. They can improve the **quality** of the **product**, reassess their methods of **promotion**, use new **pricing strategies**, and reconsider **channels** of distribution. Businesses can increase the **skills of staff** (e.g. teach hairdressers head massage techniques), make their **processes** better for the customer (e.g. make appointments bookable online), or make their **physical environment** more inviting.

- **Technological advances** are another reason why companies might change the mix. Widespread **internet** access has meant that many firms have **changed** their **method of distribution**. Also, products need to change as technology advances. E.g. computer games are now available as **digital downloads**.

- **Social factors**, such as an increasing number of pensioners, might prompt a change in a **product**, or how it is **promoted**.

- **New laws** can affect the marketing mix, e.g. a new standard for crash helmets would mean adapting **products**, and laws about how and where junk food can be advertised would change the **promotion** factor.

Practice Questions

Q1 What is the marketing mix?
Q2 List the 7Ps.
Q3 Give four influences on the marketing mix.

Exam Question

Q1 Enid owns a snack van. Her revenue has fallen since a competitor entered the market. Evaluate the changes she could make to her marketing mix to regain market share. [16 marks]

A handy tip to remember the 7Ps — they all begin with P...

The integrated marketing mix brings together the 7Ps — if a firm wants to change one of the Ps it needs to consider the impact it will have on the others. Kind of like fitting a carpet — you might try and adjust one corner to get it to fit but then a problem pops up in another corner. But enough of the carpet related analogies, you've got some work to do...

Marketing Mix — Product

There's a lot to think about before bringing a new product onto the market. Businesses need the right mix of new, growing and mature products to survive in the long-term. And the wrong product can be a pricey mistake.

There are **Three Types** of **Consumer Products**

1) **Convenience products** — these are **inexpensive**, everyday items bought **regularly** by **lots** of people. They're often bought out of **habit**, e.g. a coffee on the way to work. Consumers don't put too much thought into buying them and they don't bother shopping around for cheaper alternatives because they **wouldn't save much**.

2) **Shopping products** — these are things like clothes, computers and washing machines that are bought **less regularly** than convenience products. They're **more expensive** and are sold in **fewer places** than convenience products. People might pay more for a **particular brand**, e.g. a Bosch hob or a Jack Wills sweater.

3) **Speciality products** — these are things consumers believe are **unique** in some way, and they'll **travel** to find the exact brand — e.g. designer handbag, celebrity hair stylist or luxury car. Perceived **image** and **quality** are more important to consumers than price for speciality products, so **higher profits** can be made from them.

Businesses need a **Variety** of **Products** — a **Mixed Product Portfolio**

1) A **product line** consists of related products (including different sizes of the same product) with similar **characteristics**, **uses** or **target customers**.

2) The **product mix** is the **combination** of all the **product lines** that a business produces.

3) Businesses aim to have a **product mix** that contains a variety of different products, all at different stages of the **product life cycle** (see p.44). That way if one product fails, the business should still be able to depend on the others.

The product mix is also called the product portfolio.

The **Boston Matrix** is a model of **Portfolio Analysis**

1) The Boston Matrix compares **market growth** with **market share**. Each **circle** in the matrix represents **one product**. The **size** of each circle represents the **sales revenue** of the product.

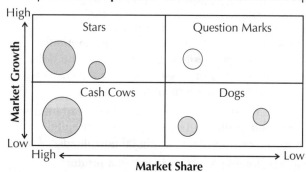

All **new products** are **question marks** (sometimes called **problem children**) and they have small market share and high market growth.
These aren't profitable yet and could succeed or fail. They need **heavy marketing** to give them a chance. A business can do various things with question marks — **brand building**, **harvesting** (maximising sales or profit in the short term) or **divestment** (selling off the product).

Cash cows have high market share but low market growth. They're in their **maturity** phase. They've already been promoted and they're produced in high volumes, so costs are low. Cash cows bring in plenty of **money**.

Stars have high market growth and high market share. They're in their profitable **growth** phase and have the **most potential**. They're future **cash cows**. BUT... competitors are likely to try to take advantage of this **growth market** too, so a firm will need to **spend** a lot on **promoting** their product to keep their **market share**. Also, money might need to be spent to **increase capacity** (see page 56) to keep up with **demand**.

Dogs have low market share and low market growth. They're usually pretty much a lost cause. If they're still profitable, e.g. a chocolate bar that is still popular, but no longer growing, the business will **harvest profit** in the **short term**. If the product is no longer making a profit it can be **sold off**.

Jack had low growth — so he tried standing on two legs to make himself look taller.

2) The **Boston Matrix** is a **valuable** way of showing where a business's products are **positioned** in the market.

3) A business's marketing **decisions** will depend on the products' **positions** in the matrix. For example, a business can use money from its **cash cows** to **invest** in its **question marks** so they can become **stars**.

4) But the Boston Matrix **can't predict exactly** what will happen to a product. A product's **profit** may be **different** from what the matrix suggests (e.g. a dog can have strong cash flow and be profitable despite falling sales).

Marketing Mix — Product

New Products can be great for a business

There are three main reasons why it is worthwhile for companies to develop new products:

1) New products can bring in **new customers**.
2) They give a **competitive** advantage.
3) They allow companies to maintain a **balanced product portfolio**.

Competition and Technology can inspire New Products

Most new products come about for one of three reasons:

1) **Technological developments** mean that a company can now offer the customer something that it couldn't offer before, e.g. 3D TV. In the long term, the new product is likely to be a **replacement** for the old one.

2) A company might develop an **imitative** new product in response to one which has been launched by a **competitor**, e.g. lots of companies decided to develop bagless vacuum cleaners after the launch of the Dyson™.

3) Somebody within the company (usually the owner or a manager) identifies a **gap in the market** for an **innovative** product. Products such as The Sony WALKMAN® or 3M's Post-it® Notes originally fitted into this category. In order to create **innovative products**, companies have to spend lots on **research and development (R&D)**. It is a **high risk** strategy but also carries the **highest potential rewards**.

New Products need a Unique Selling Point (USP)

Every successful new product, whether it is innovative, imitative or a replacement for an existing product, needs to have something that **differentiates** it from the **competition**. This is known as a **Unique Selling Point** or a **Unique Selling Proposition (USP)**. USPs can be **tangible benefits** and **intangible benefits**.

1) **Tangible benefits** can be **measured**. Products with tangible benefits that could be used as USPs are things like low-calorie pizza, energy-efficient fridges and savings accounts with high rates of interest.

2) **Intangible benefits** are things that **can't be measured**. They're based on concepts such as reputation and product image. E.g. beauty products market themselves as making the consumer **feel good** and certain makes of car are perceived as being **reliable**.

3) A product's tangible and intangible benefits are important, but there are other things the consumer considers. These might be things like **customer service**, **money-back guarantees**, and availability of **spare parts**.

4) **Service** businesses need USPs too. E.g. Butlins, a chain of holiday camps, claim that so much is included in the price that you won't have to spend any extra money while you're there.

Jim had read the whole manual, but he still couldn't find his laptop's USP.

Practice Questions

Q1 What are the three types of consumer product?

Q2 Sketch and label the Boston Matrix.

Q3 Explain why the Boston Matrix is a valuable tool for portfolio analysis.

Q4 What is the benefit for a company of having a product with a unique selling point?

Exam Questions

Q1 Explain why a small company which is new to the market might prefer to launch an imitative, rather than innovative, product. [4 marks]

Q2 Discuss the usefulness of the Boston Matrix to a biscuit manufacturer. [9 marks]

Glitches in the Boston Matrix create Cash Dogs...

It's really important for a business to have a balanced product portfolio — lots of cash cows might seem like a good thing but the business will worry that the market is growing too slowly and that there are no extra sales to be made from those products. Having lots of stars isn't really a problem though, as long as you can maintain their market share...

Marketing Mix — Product

All products are born with no sales at all. If they're looked after, they grow into big strong products with lots of sales, then they get married and have lots of spin-offs ... er, maybe.

Products *have a* Life Cycle

1) The product life cycle shows the **sales** of a product over **time**.

2) It's **valuable** for planning **marketing strategies** and changing the **marketing mix**.

3) **Marketing decisions** will be based on where a product is in its **life cycle** (see next page).

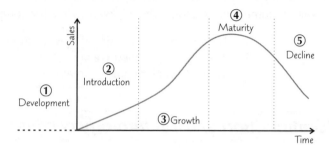

1 — Development

1) The **research and development** (R&D) department **develop** the product.

2) The **marketing** department does **market research**.

3) The **costs** are **high**, and there aren't any sales yet to cover the costs.

4) Development has a **high failure rate**. This is because there's often **not enough demand**, or because the business can't make the product **cheaply** enough to make a profit.

2 — Introduction

1) The product is **launched**, either in one market or in several markets. It's sometimes launched with **complementary** products — e.g. the PlayStation® was launched with games.

2) The business often **promotes** the product heavily to build sales — but businesses need to make sure they've got enough **resources** and **capacity** to **meet the demand** that promotions create.

3) The **initial price** of the product may be **high** to cover **promotional costs**. This is called **skimming**.

4) Alternatively, the price can start off **low** to encourage sales. This is **penetration pricing**.

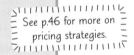

See p.46 for more on pricing strategies.

5) Sales go up, but the sales revenue has to pay for the high **fixed cost** of development **before** the product can make a **profit**. The business usually ditches products with disappointing sales after this stage.

6) There aren't many **outlets** for the new product — businesses have to work hard to persuade retailers to sell it.

7) Competition may be **limited** (if it's an **innovative** product).

3 — Growth

1) Sales grow fast. There are **new customers** and **repeat** customers.

2) **Competitors** may be attracted to the market. Promotion shows **differences** from the competitors' products.

3) The product is often **improved** or **developed**, and it may be targeted at a different market segment.

4) Rising sales encourage **more outlets** to stock the product.

4 — Maturity

1) **Sales** reach a **peak** and profitability increases because **fixed costs** of **development** have been **paid for**.

2) At **saturation** (when the market is full and has reached maximum growth) sales may begin to drop, depending on the product. Sales are more likely to drop for long-lasting products that customers do not need to replace regularly. The price is often reduced to stimulate **demand**, which reduces profits.

3) There aren't many new customers. **Competition** within the industry becomes fierce so sales might **suffer**.

5 — Decline

1) The product doesn't **appeal** to customers any more. **Sales fall** rapidly and profits decrease.

2) On the other hand, the product may stay profitable if **promotional costs** are **reduced** enough.

3) If sales carry on falling, the product is **withdrawn** or **sold** to another business (**divestment**). Sometimes, sales might pick up again if competitors leave the market first.

Marketing Mix — Product

Extension Strategies keep a product Going Strong for Longer

Extension strategies try to prolong the life of the product by changing the **marketing mix**. They include:

1) **Product development** — businesses **improve**, reformulate or **redesign** a product. They can change the design of **packaging** to make it look more up to date, or make **special editions** of the product. This can also give a **new focus** to existing **marketing** campaigns.

2) **Market development** — businesses can find **new markets** or **new uses** for existing products. They can aim an existing product at a new market **segment** (e.g. Hunter® boots are now marketed as a fashion item as well as practical outdoor footwear).

3) A business can change the way the product's **distributed** — by selling through the **internet**, selling through **supermarkets** or convenience stores, etc. Alternatively, they could try marketing it in a **different country**.

4) A business can change the way the product's **priced**, or use special offers or competitions.

5) A business can change the way they **promote** the product — by running a new **ad campaign**, for example.

> **Decline isn't inevitable** — it's usually caused by products becoming obsolete, changing consumer tastes or poor marketing. Quality products with excellent original design (e.g. Cadbury Dairy Milk) can carry on selling for **decades**.

The Product Life Cycle is Valuable when changing the Marketing Mix

1) Businesses need to know what stage of the **product life cycle** a product is at in order to **adapt** the marketing mix correctly. Their marketing **decisions** are partly based on the **product life cycle**.

2) When a product is in **development**, the focus should be on **product** and **price** — marketing can do research into what **product** people **want** and **how much** people are willing to **pay** for it. In the final stages of development, the marketing mix changes may start to focus on **how** they are going to **promote** it and **where** they are going to **sell it**.

3) As the product is first **introduced**, marketing usually focuses heavily on **place** and **promotion** to get the product out there and raise awareness of it. Marketing also need to think about training **people** to be more **knowledgeable** about the product. Depending on how well the product is received, the **price** might be adjusted.

4) As the product enters the **growth** stage, the marketing mix may be more focused on **people, physical environment** and **process**. People will need to be **well-trained** to deal with queries from new customers and the company can also be more picky about the **physical environment** (e.g. they might redesign their website). The **process** has to be improved to keep the additional customers happy with the service they are receiving.

5) During the **maturity** stage of the life cycle, the marketing mix may focus on **price** and **promotion** again. The **price** of the product can be reduced and the unique features of the product can be **promoted** in order to stay competitive. Marketing might look at **adapting the product** to keep their sales up for as long as possible.

6) When sales of the product begin to **decline**, marketing will decrease the amount of money they spend on each of the 7Ps. **Promotion** may stop altogether, **discounted prices** will be offered, the product may be **pulled out** of some stores and they will **stop training** people.

Practice Questions

Q1 What are the stages of the product life cycle?

Q2 Why does profitability increase in the maturity phase of the product's life cycle?

Q3 What are extension strategies?

Q4 How does the promotion of a product change during its life cycle?

Exam Question

Q1 A software developer is ready to launch a new computer game.
Evaluate the possible impact of the life cycle of the game on its marketing mix. [16 marks]

No product can live for ever — except maybe the wheel...

There's a lot to learn on these pages, I'll give you that. If you take it step by step though, it's fairly straightforward — it really just goes through the different stages in the life cycle of a product. And if you know the product life cycle inside out, it won't be so hard to learn the other bits mentioned here about extension strategies, the 7Ps and so on.

Marketing Mix — Pricing

The basic rules of pricing are obvious — a firm needs to price its product so that it covers its costs but is still affordable for the consumer. Products often change price at different stages in their life cycle.

Several Factors affect Pricing Decisions

1) The **price** of a product is affected by all of the other Ps in the **marketing mix** — e.g. during heavy **promotion** of a product, its **price** may be **reduced**.

2) The price is often set to **cover the cost** of making the product (or buying it from a wholesaler) and **make a profit**. This is called **cost-plus pricing**. The percentage amount that's added on to the cost is called the **mark-up**.

3) The price must be **acceptable to customers** — it depends how **price sensitive** the target market is. Affluent consumers are less price sensitive than those at the other end of the scale.

4) The **price elasticity of demand** (see page 36) influences the pricing of a product. This depends on the **availability of substitutes**, the **type** of product, the **age** of the product, whether it's an **expensive purchase**, and **loyalty** to the brand.

5) The stage of the **product's life cycle** (see page 44) will also affect pricing decisions — for example, if sales are declining then price may be **reduced**.

6) The price has to be in line with the company's **objectives**. E.g. they might be aiming to increase their **market share**, make the **maximum profit**, or keep their **brand image** up-market.

7) The price of **competitor products** influences pricing decisions. If the price is set **above** that of competitor products without it being **differentiated** in some way then no one will buy it and it may bring the company **bad publicity**. However, if the price is too far **below** that of others, particularly the major players', then customers will question its **quality**.

No one was sure which was falling faster — Jim, or demand for tiny swimming trunks.

Companies use Promotional Pricing Strategies for New Products

Price Skimming

1) **Price skimming** is when **new** and **innovative products** are sold at **high prices** when they first reach the market. Consumers will pay more because the product has **scarcity value**, and the high price boosts the **product's image** and increases its appeal. **Technological products**, e.g. computers, tend to be priced using this method.

2) Prices are usually then **dropped considerably** when the product has been on the market for a year or so — by this point everyone prepared to pay extra for being one of the first to own the product has got one. Also, competitors will have entered the market with **imitative products** at **lower prices** — unless a company can prevent this by using **patents** or **trademarks**.

3) Some companies use price skimming as a **long term strategy** to keep their brands **more exclusive**, e.g. Apple® and Ray-Ban® sunglasses.

4) However, **potential customers** can be put off by the initial high price and customers who bought the product at its initial price may be **annoyed** and **frustrated** when it suddenly drops in price after launch.

Penetration Pricing

1) **Penetration pricing** is the opposite of skimming. It means launching a product at a **low price** in order to **attract customers** and gain **market share**. It is especially effective in markets which are **price-sensitive**, e.g. a new washing powder or food product.

2) Penetration pricing works best for companies that can benefit from **lower costs** when manufacturing **large quantities** of a product.

3) A **problem** with penetration pricing is that customers expect the low price to **continue**, so it's difficult to raise it without losing customers. It can also damage how the **brand image** is perceived.

4) Price penetration isn't just for new products — it can be used as an **extension strategy** to prolong a product's life (see page 45).

5) Penetration can also be used to target a more **budget-conscious** market segment. E.g. an airline might set up a **no-frills, low-cost service** in addition to its regular service. That way they can keep their **existing customer base** who are prepared to pay more, as well as maintaining their premium brand image.

Marketing Mix — Pricing

There are lots of other **Pricing Strategies**

1) **Predatory pricing** is when a business **deliberately lowers prices** to force another business **out of the market** (which is illegal under EU and US laws) — e.g. a large nationwide company might target a successful but small local competitor by lowering their prices in that specific area until the small competitor **goes out of business**. Once the competitor has gone they will **raise** their prices again.

2) **Competitive pricing** is when companies **monitor** their **competitors' prices** to make sure that their own prices are set at an equal or lower level. **Supermarkets** and **department stores** often use this method. Some stores will **refund the difference** in price if the product is cheaper somewhere else.

3) **Psychological pricing** bases the price on customers' **expectations**. A **high price** may make people think the product is really **high quality**. An **insignificant** price change can have a big **psychological impact** on the customer, e.g. £99.99 seems a lot better than £100 even though it's only 1p difference.

4) **Loss leaders** are products sold at or below cost price. These products may well **lose money**, but the idea is that they'll **make a profit** for the business **indirectly** anyway, e.g. by enticing customers into the shop where they'll probably buy full-priced items too. The loss leaders can be widely **advertised** to encourage this. This tactic can work well in **supermarkets**, where customers will usually buy lots of **other items** as well as the loss leader.

5) **Price discrimination** is when a company sells its product at different prices to **different groups of consumers**. E.g. zoo ticket prices often vary according to the **age** of the customer.

Dynamic Pricing responds to **Changes In Demand**

1) Dynamic pricing aims to increase revenue by changing prices depending on **competitor prices** and **demand**.

2) Hotel rooms, air travel and rail tickets are often dynamically priced. Prices change as the **travel date** gets **nearer**. They can also change according to the **day** or **time** that a customer wants to travel.

3) If demand is **high** at a particular time, prices **rise**, and if demand is **low**, prices go **down**. It also allows firms to make **increased profit** at busy times and offset some of the costs of having **excess capacity** during quiet periods (as well as creating **extra demand** at these times).

Industrial Marketing has Different **Pricing Influences**

1) Many businesses sell to **other businesses** rather than directly to consumers. E.g. photocopier companies market their products to businesses, brake suppliers market their products to bike manufacturers.

2) When businesses are selling to other businesses they try to build a **good ongoing relationship** with the customer, which may be worth **sacrificing** some immediate **profit** for. They want the customer to make **repeat purchases** and they might be able to make **extra profit** by providing spare parts and servicing.

3) Like with consumer marketing, **price** depends on the **competitiveness** of the market.

4) Other parts of the **marketing mix** differ in industrial marketing too. E.g. **promotions** tend to be less persuasive and more **informative** as business buyers will be more **knowledgeable** and **objective**.

5) **Place** will also differ, e.g. **trade shows** are important for industrial marketing.

Practice Questions

Q1 What are price skimming and price penetration?

Q2 Give an example of dynamic pricing.

Q3 What influences pricing in industrial marketing?

Exam Questions

Q1 Explain why a hotel might use dynamic pricing for its rooms. [4 marks]

Q2 A small company is launching a new brand of fruit juice. Suggest a pricing strategy it should consider, and analyse the advantages and disadvantages of this strategy. [9 marks]

Price skimming — a way of milking profits...

When it comes to pricing, most companies use a cost-based method and throw in the occasional bit of promotional pricing to keep consumers interested. But remember — price isn't the only thing that bothers customers...

Marketing Mix — Promotion

Promotion — basically it means using advertising, branding, sales promotion and PR to sell more products.

Promotion is part of the Marketing Mix

1) Promotion is designed to **inform** customers about a product or service, or **persuade** them to buy it. **Industrial promotion** tends to be **informative**, whereas **consumer promotion** tends to be **persuasive**.

2) **Promotional objectives** include increasing **sales** and **profits**, and increasing **awareness** of the product.

3) All promotion has to get the customer's **attention** so that they can be informed or persuaded about the product.

Many companies choose to Advertise through the Media

1) Adverts are used to **promote goods** and **services** — and also to promote a firm's **public image**. Advertising uses various **media** including print, film, TV, radio, billboards (also called hoardings) and the Internet.

2) The choice of media depends on the **number of target customers** and how many of them **see** the ad. TV adverts at prime times are very expensive. Ads shown when fewer people are watching are cheaper, but don't reach as many people. The cost must be **worth it** in terms of the **extra sales** or **awareness** created.

3) **Digital advertising** is **cheaper** than traditional forms:

> - Businesses can **target** online adverts to customers who've shown an **interest** in that type of product by browsing for it online.
> - **Advertising** on **mobile phones** is becoming increasingly important, e.g. banners in apps — sometimes the advertiser is only charged when their advert is **clicked on**, so no money is wasted on unseen ads.
> - **Viral marketing** is when companies get users to **pass on adverts** to their friends through social networking platforms or email, etc. The adverts have to be considered **interesting enough** for people to pass along, e.g. a hilarious video, or something that offers something for **free**.

The TV remote — scourge of TV advertisers everywhere.

4) The **impact** of an ad is very important. An advert that covers a two-page spread in a magazine has much more impact than a single page, or a small ad stuck in the classified section at the back.

5) **Specialist media** are used to advertise specialist products to **niche markets**. For example, a manufacturer of fish hooks would do better to advertise in a monthly fishing magazine than in the Daily Telegraph newspaper.

6) Companies need to follow **legal constraints** on advertising some products. E.g. cigarette advertising is banned.

Advertising changes during a Product Life Cycle

See p.44-45 for more on product life cycles.

1) Products are often heavily advertised at **launch**. If a product is completely **new** to the market, the adverts are **informative**. They tell customers about the product.

2) During the **growth** phase, advertising **differentiates** between brands, persuading consumers that the product is better than competitor products. The objective during this phase is to **maintain** or **increase market share**.

3) When a product is at the **mature**, **saturation** phase, consumers need to be **reminded** of it. If the manufacturer has an **extension** strategy, they can use advertising to inform consumers about, say, any **improvements** to the product.

Branding is a key aspect of Product Image

Branding differentiates a product from the competition. Customers recognise it through its name, logo or slogan. Brands can be **individual** products, e.g. Sprite®, or "family brands" covering a **range** of products, e.g. Heinz®.

1) If a business convinces customers that their brand is **superior** to others, they can charge a **premium price**.

2) Customers often remain **loyal** to a brand as they have **confidence** in its quality. New products launched under the same brand will often be **accepted more readily**, without much being spent on promotion.

3) Packaging is important to **distinguish** the product, e.g. the Coca-Cola® bottle. This is more true for some products than others, e.g. **fancy chocolates** need attractive packaging, but bulk orders of **printer toner** don't.

4) Popular brands often **eliminate competition** and **deter new competitors**. If there are no alternative products, then the price will become **inelastic** and can be **increased** without reducing demand much.

5) Some brand names have an **ethical** or **environmentally-friendly** image. The companies behind them aim to appeal to consumers concerned about these issues.

Marketing Mix — Promotion

Not All promotion involves Advertising

1) Companies often offer **sales promotions**. These are things like **special offers**, e.g. "buy one get one free" (**BOGOF)**, competitions and free gifts. Sales promotions can aim to **raise awareness** or **increase sales** of a product. Manufacturers also aim sales promotions at the **retailer** to encourage them to **stock** more of their products.

2) **Merchandising** means ensuring that retailers are displaying a company's products as effectively as possible. Some merchandisers offer retailers **point of sale displays** (e.g. special colourful racks with the company logo).

3) **Direct mail** means **mailshots** sent out to customers. The customer usually hasn't **asked** to receive them. Businesses that keep information about their customers on a database can **target** their direct mail to particular consumer groups either through post or email. Direct mail that is untargeted ("**junk mail**") can sometimes be a **waste of money**, because it often just gets thrown away.

4) **Personal selling** or **direct selling** is personal communication between a **salesperson** and a customer. Personal selling can involve sales assistants in shops as well as travelling salespeople and phone salespeople.

5) **Relationship marketing** involves forming **long-term relationships** with customers. This costs **less** in marketing than continually attracting new customers. For example, a business could offer existing customers **special offers** or **loyalty cards**. **Social media** is very useful for **relationship-building** with customers.

6) **Event sponsorship** makes consumers **aware** of a firm and its product. It also gives the firm a **good image**.

7) **Direct Response TV Marketing** encourages consumers to contact the advertiser directly to purchase a product they have seen advertised on television. **Shopping channels** are an example of this kind of promotion.

PR gets businesses or products Good Publicity in the Media

1) **Public relations** (**PR**) involves **liaising** with the **media**, writing **press releases**, and answering **press enquiries**.

2) PR departments write **brochures**, **newsletters** and **leaflets** giving information about the company.

3) Public relations deals with things like **product launches**, **conferences** and other **special events**.

The Promotional Mix reflects Product, Budget and Competitor Activity

1) Businesses use a **mixture** of methods to promote products. This is called the **promotional mix**.

2) The promotional mix depends on: the **product** itself, the **market**, **competitor activity**, the **product life cycle** and the **budget** available.

3) In general, **convenience** products purchased by the **consumer** are promoted by **advertising**.

4) **Expensive** and **complex** products are more likely to be promoted by **personal selling**. So are products or services sold in the **industrial market**.

See p.42 for more on convenience, shopping and speciality products.

5) **Shopping products**, e.g. perfumes and bikes, and **speciality products**, e.g. luxury cars, are often sold by a combination of **advertising** and **personal selling**. TV, print and billboard adverts **attract the buyer** into the showroom, where the salesperson takes over.

6) Manufacturers use different methods to sell their product to a **retailer** than to sell it to the **final customer**. Businesses often use **salespeople** to get **shops** to stock their product, and **advertising** to persuade **customers** to buy the product in the shops.

7) The promotional mix reflects the **economy**. E.g. in a **recession**, McDonald's may promote their 'Saver Menu'.

Practice Questions

Q1 What is promotion designed to do?

Q2 In which phase of the product life cycle does advertising stress differences with competitor products?

Q3 Give three ways that branding helps a company maximise its sales.

Exam Question

Q1 Analyse how, in addition to advertising, a manufacturer of breakfast cereal could promote its product. [9 marks]

We want people to buy our product — that's why we tell them to BOGOF...

When it comes to promotion, it's all in the mix. You'll need to suggest which combination of methods would best suit a firm, and why. The optimum mix for a product will change depending on where it is in its life cycle.

Marketing Mix — Place

Distribution is important. This is the "place" part of the marketing mix. If a product can't get to the marketplace, no one can buy it. Needs go unfulfilled, companies don't make profits, anarchy reigns...

It's **Vital** to get the **Product** to the **Consumer**

A **channel** of **distribution** is the route a product takes from the producer to the consumer. A product usually passes through **intermediaries** on the way from producer to consumer — e.g. **retailers**, **wholesalers** and **agents**.

1) **Retailers** are **shops** who sell to consumers. They're usually the **final stage** in the distribution channel. Tesco, Argos and amazon® are **retailers**. Retailers can be physical shops or online "e-tailers".

2) **Wholesalers** buy products cheaply in **bulk** (particularly convenience items) and **sell them on** to **retailers**. Wholesalers make life **easier** for retailers and manufacturers:

   • Wholesalers **buy** goods from manufacturers in bulk and **sell** them in **smaller quantities** to **retailers**. This is called "**breaking bulk**" — a wholesaler takes the goods off the manufacturer's hands and **pays** for the whole lot. Manufacturers don't have to **wait** for customers to buy the goods before they see any cash.

   • Wholesalers make distribution **simpler**. Without a wholesaler, the manufacturer would have to make **separate deliveries** to lots of retailers, and send each and every retailer an **invoice**. Selling to one wholesaler cuts down the paperwork and the number of journeys.

   • Wholesalers can **store more goods** than a retailer can — they act as the retailer's storage cupboard.

There are **Different Channels** of **Distribution**

Direct Selling (0-level channel): Manufacturer ⇒ Consumer

The **Internet** has made it **easier** for producers of **shopping** and **speciality** goods to sell **direct** to the consumer. Buying and selling on the Internet is called **e-commerce**. This allows access to a **worldwide market**. For small firms, a low-cost option is to sell goods using **electronic marketplaces** (e.g. eBay®). **Direct selling** is done through door-to-door sales, TV shopping channels, telephone sales and websites. Accountants, electricians and hairdressers sell their **services** direct to the consumer.

Indirect Selling (1-level channel): Manufacturer ⇒ Retailer ⇒ Consumer

Large supermarkets buy **convenience** and **shopping** goods in bulk direct from the manufacturer and have them delivered straight from the manufacturer or via their own warehouses. This is a faster method for **perishables**.

Direct Selling through an agent (1-level channel): Manufacturer ⇒ Agent ⇒ Consumer

An **agent** is like a **sales representative**, except they are **not employed** by the company whose goods they sell. They get **commission** (a percentage of the value of the goods they sell) instead of being paid a **salary**. E.g. Avon products are sold by **agents** who sell Avon products in their own name rather than as an Avon employee.

Indirect Selling (2-level channel): Manufacturer ⇒ Wholesaler ⇒ Retailer ⇒ Consumer

This is the **traditional** distribution channel used for **convenience goods**, e.g. by fast-food chains.

Retailers often use **Multi-Channel Distribution**

Multi-channel distribution is when businesses sell through more than one method, e.g. online and in store. It gives **flexibility** for customers and a **wide market coverage** for manufacturers.

1) Supermarkets and fashion retailers which have **high street stores** as well as an **internet store** are using a **multi-channel strategy**. This may lead to added costs, but it allows them to target a wider market.

2) Stores which **only** sell **online** may have **cheaper costs**, because they use a **single** channel of distribution. However, they can have **problems** establishing **brand loyalty**. Also, customers often like to see and feel goods before they buy them, which is a **limitation of e-commerce**.

> **Example:** Apple® uses multi-channel distribution. You can buy an iPad® **directly** from an **Apple® Store**, either **online** or in a **physical shop**. Alternatively, you can buy it from an **online retailer** such as amazon®, or from a retailer such as ASDA or PC World, either **online** or from a **retail outlet**...

Marketing Mix — Place

Businesses choose a *Channel* of *Distribution* to *Suit Their Needs*

The choice of distribution channel is a compromise between **cost**, **ease** and **control**.

1) It's **more profitable** to **sell direct** to the customer. Each intermediary (party) in the distribution chain takes a **slice of profit** from the manufacturer — wholesalers and retailers have to make money too. Businesses that **sell direct** can offer their product at a **lower price** than **retailers** at the end of a long distribution chain.

2) On the other hand, it's **easier** to use **intermediaries**, especially for convenience goods. It'd be a hassle to distribute a small amount of product to lots of little shops. It's easier to sell to a **wholesaler** who can deliver products from several manufacturers in a single delivery. Using wholesalers often means more **market coverage**.

3) The **fewer intermediaries** in the distribution chain, the more **control** a manufacturer has over how its products are sold. It has more say in the **final selling price** and how the product is **promoted**. For example, some companies aim to **protect** their brand's up-market image by not allowing it to be sold in supermarkets.

4) UK **retail trends** have **changed** in recent years, as retailers have found **cheaper** or **more effective** ways of distributing their products. **Out-of-town retail parks**, **concessions** (shops within shops), and **mail-order catalogues** have **cheaper overheads** than high street stores and often offer customers other **benefits**, such as **free parking**. **Factory outlets** allow firms to make a return on **imperfect goods** (seconds) or **last season's stock**.

Short Distribution Channels	Long Distribution Channels
• Industrial products	• Consumer products
• Few customers	• Many customers
• Expensive, complex goods	• Inexpensive, simple goods
• Infrequent sales	• Frequent sales
• Bespoke (custom-made) products	• Standard products
• Bulky products	• Small products
• Services	• Goods

There are no real hard and fast rules about which distribution channel a business might choose, but there are a few trends.

The **choices** of distribution channels for **new** and **small business** can be **limited** as they struggle to place their products **directly** into major chains. They might have to sell through established **agents** or **wholesalers**, which will directly impact on their profits.

A product's place *Within an Outlet* is important too

1) Manufacturers try to influence retailers to give their products more **prominence**. E.g. a drinks manufacturer might supply a fridge with their **branding** all over it. Leading brands such as Kelloggs® and Coca-Cola® create lots of **product varieties** to get more **shelf space** and squeeze out the competition.

2) Supermarkets use tactics to get you to buy more — e.g. they put **everyday essentials** such as bread and milk at the back so you have to walk through the **whole shop** and are tempted to buy **other products** on the way.

3) In e-commerce, businesses try to get their product to appear at the **top** of the lists on e.g. amazon® or Google™. They do this by including **keywords** in their description and getting lots of **positive customer ratings**.

Practice Questions

Q1 What is the role of a wholesaler?

Q2 Describe two distribution channels.

Q3 Why do businesses often use multi-channel distribution?

Exam Questions

Q1 Analyse the possible influences on the choice of distribution channel for a firm selling clothes aimed at young people. [9 marks]

Q2 Evaluate e-commerce as a means of distributing luxury consumer goods. [12 marks]

I'm a new product — get me out of here...

Distribution can seem like a mundane, boring thing. Yes, it is all about warehouses full of cardboard boxes, fleets of trucks going from A to B and people popping catalogues through your letterbox. But on the other hand it's a vital part of the wondrous marketing mix. Where you can buy something is a big factor in deciding whether to buy it.

People, Process and Physical Environment

You are probably a bit P'd out, but there's still the final three Ps to go. As the service sector now dominates the UK's economic activity, these final Ps have been added as they're super-relevant to service businesses.

People are a Vital Part of providing Goods and Services

1) With **services** such as banking, hairdressing and dining out, the customer's experience is highly dependent on the **people** dealing with them. E.g. an attentive waiter with a good knowledge of the menu will make a customer's experience far more enjoyable. Sometimes the person is the **only aspect** of a service a customer sees — e.g. they might not be able to see the work done on their central heating pipes, but most customers would prefer to use a pleasant plumber who explains things well.

2) If employees are **friendly, polite and knowledgeable**, people are **more likely** to buy the goods or service from them, **promote** them by word-of-mouth and **return** again and again — so it makes sense for businesses to focus on providing excellent **customer service**. The **Internet** makes this aspect really important as customers will often put a **review** of their experience online.

3) When you buy things in a shop, you'll usually be served by a **person**, but some **goods** have more of a service element — e.g. someone buying a child car seat might go into a **specialist shop** and seek **advice** on the best seat for their needs and be shown how to fit it correctly. If you buy a computer, you might need **after-sales personnel** to help you set it up. People are an **important** part of the customer's experience.

4) In **e-commerce**, customers can usually enquire about a product either through **e-mail** or by **phone**. Getting a **prompt, knowledgeable** reply to an e-mail will encourage a customer to **buy** the product and **review** the company favourably.

5) For **business customers**, access to someone who can explain **technical aspects** of the product is important. Also, business-to-business **sales people** need to have the **interpersonal skills** to form **good ongoing relationships** with business customers.

The *Process is the System* of providing *Goods and Services* to customers

The **process** is how easy it is for customers to get **what they want**, **when they want it**.
It's the customers' **experience** of the business. Some **process** elements that concern customers are:

> - How easy is it to get an **appointment** at a time that suits them?
> - How long do they have to wait? E.g. for their food in a restaurant.
> - Are the advertised products **in stock**?
> - What **payment methods** are available?
> - How **user-friendly** is the **website**?
> - What **after-sales service** is offered — e.g. is the builder's work **guaranteed**?
> - Will a **phone enquiry** be answered by a person or a machine?
> - How **quickly** will a business respond to complaints?

Kevin the koala won the cuteness selection process.

1) Businesses have to **decide** how to **balance** maximising profits while keeping customers happy with their processes. E.g. in a call centre it is convenient for operators to put customers **on hold** during periods of **high demand** — however, **customers** can get **annoyed** if they are waiting for too long.

2) Different businesses place **different degrees of importance** on processes. E.g. ASDA has invested in hybrid tills which can be operated by a member of staff or as a self-service till so all the checkouts are always open and queues are kept short. Whereas Aldi places more emphasis on low prices than on short queues.

3) Process aspects can be used in **promotion**. E.g. an online retailer might advertise 'next day delivery as standard'.

4) **Technology** can be used to improve processes. For example:

> **Queue management technology** is used by **airports** to direct customers to **shorter queues** and inform them how long their waiting time will be — known waits seem shorter than unknown waits.
>
> Lots of e-tailers offer the option to **pay through PayPal**, meaning customers can use their **address** and **payment details** already linked to their PayPal account.

5) In **e-commerce**, good processes are important. Customers will leave **feedback** about how promptly their product arrived, and how well any **complaints** were dealt with. Also, the **ranking** (how close to the top the product features) on sites such as amazon®, is affected by things like how **quickly** goods are shipped, how often the product is **out of stock** and how often the product is **returned**.

People, Process and Physical Environment

Physical Environment is the customer's Surroundings

1) **Physical environment** includes things like:

- **Decor and cleanliness** — the decor should fit in with the **nature** of the business.
  Cleanliness is important in **all** businesses, especially **restaurants** and **hotels**.
- **Appearance of the website** — a good website should reflect the business's **nature** and **ethics**.
  A professional-looking website will create a good impression of the business.
- **Appearance of staff** — businesses can give customers an **impression** of the business through the
  appearance of their staff, e.g. they could be dressed **casually**, **smartly**, in **uniform**, etc.
- **Layout** — how easy it is to **find your way around** a physical location or a website. Customers can
  get **annoyed** if they can't find the item they want, so they might use **another store** or **website** instead.
- **Practicality and safety** — customers need to have **access** to the products and be able to **purchase**
  them **safely** — for example, heavy goods shouldn't be on the top shelf in a supermarket.

2) The physical environment can **influence** whether a customer buys goods or services from the business.
   For example, a travel agent might have a **modern**, **clean** and **stylish** office to give customers the
   impression that their holidays will be up to the same standards.

3) The physical environment can also give an **impression** of the **nature** of the business.
   For example, banks often have **neutral decor** and look very **clean** to reflect the **seriousness**
   of the business — staff wear **uniforms** or **suits** so that the bank comes across as **professional**.

Businesses make Decisions about these 3Ps

As part of an **integrated** marketing mix, **decisions** about people, process and physical environment
depend on the **type** of product and the **other elements** of the mix.

Decisions about the 3Ps at a luxury hotel and a budget hotel

A **luxury hotel** needs to provide a **high quality experience** that customers are willing to pay a **high price** for,
whereas a **budget hotel** will aim to **minimise** their **costs** to allow them to offer **cheaper prices**.

- **People** — a luxury hotel will want to hire the **best staff** possible, and **train** them to an even higher
  standard. For example, they will want experienced, quality chefs. A budget hotel will hire staff
  who are less experienced or less qualified — this usually means that they will be paid a **lower wage**.
- **Process** — a luxury hotel will offer a **high level of care** throughout your visit. For example,
  staff will carry your bags to your room, clean and tidy daily, provide room service, etc.
  A budget hotel might offer more of a **no-frills service** to keep their costs down.
- **Physical environment** — a luxury hotel will consider their **physical location** and **decor** very carefully
  to make sure it **appeals** to their **target market**. For example, they might choose a large country estate,
  or **prime location** in a city, and will have **expensive** decoration, whereas a budget hotel might be in a
  slightly **less convenient location** and might concentrate more on a clean, neutral look.

Practice Questions

Q1 Explain why it is worthwhile for a business to recruit suitable people.
Q2 Give three examples of process elements that matter to customers.
Q3 How can businesses use technology to improve processes?
Q4 Give five aspects of the physical environment that businesses need to think about.

Exam Questions

Q1 How important do you think the physical environment is likely to be to a café? Justify your answer. [16 marks]

Q2 Evaluate the effect of people, process and physical environment on the other
elements of the integrated marketing mix for a national hairdressing chain. [16 marks]

Business, GSOH, seeks customers for long-term relationship...

*It's hard to split things up into 'purely goods' and 'purely services'. Most 'goods' businesses have an element of
'service', and many 'service' businesses sell something too — e.g. hairdressers sell shampoo, etc. Anyway, it's the
service elements these P's are most important for. Just don't forget them when you're talking about the marketing mix.*

Operational Objectives

This section might sound complicated, but actually, it's not. 'Operations' is just a fancy word for the real reason businesses exist in the first place — to make stuff.

Operational Objectives are Targets set for Production

Setting operational objectives can help a company achieve its **overall objectives** (see p.3-5) — operational **decisions** will become **focused** on meeting these objectives. The **performance** of the production department can be **reviewed** and **assessed** on its ability to meet these operational objectives:

QUALITY — This type of objective is likely to involve either **maintaining** or **improving** levels of quality. For example, a company might aim to ensure that **95%** of their products last **five years** or longer, or they might aim to **reduce** the number of **customer complaints** that they get in a month.

COSTS — Many firms aim to **cut costs**, especially if they compete on **price**. Depending on the type of business, there are different ways of doing this. The firm can cut its **fixed costs** or **variable costs** (see p.6) — e.g. the firm might **restructure** to remove a layer of management, or the costs of an individual **product** can be reduced (e.g. an airline might stop offering meals on a particular route).

FLEXIBILITY — Businesses need to be able to **react** to what customers want. For example, they need to be able to vary the **amount** of goods or services that they are producing so that **volume** doesn't **exceed demand** or vice-versa. E.g. if a business knows people buy fewer healthy choice ready-meals at Christmas, it might reduce production in December. Some companies ensure their workforce is flexible by employing people on **zero-hours contracts**.

Zero-hours contracts are when a worker is employed without a guaranteed minimum number of hours per week.

EFFICIENCY — Efficiency objectives aim to make **better use** of **resources** in order to reduce costs and increase profit. This might mean increasing **capacity utilisation** (increasing output so it's closer to the maximum amount of goods the firm could produce with current levels of staff and machinery) or taking steps to improve **labour** and **capital productivity** (how much output a particular worker or piece of machinery generates in a set time period).

See p.56-57 for more on capacity utilisation.

INNOVATION — Businesses can set their **Research & Development** (R&D) department innovation targets, e.g. a car manufacturer might set an objective to produce a zero-emissions car by 2018. These objectives can be **hard** to **achieve**, as unexpected problems often occur.

ENVIRONMENT — **Pressure** from **customers** and the **Government** often leads to firms setting environmental objectives, such as cutting **carbon emissions** or using a greater number of **recycled** raw materials.

SPEED OF RESPONSE — The **speed** at which a business can operate is important. This might mean decreasing the **production time** of a product, decreasing the **waiting time** for customers or getting new products to market **more quickly**. These objectives are often closely related to the company's **efficiency** objectives.

DEPENDABILITY — Customers need to be able to depend on a **business** and businesses need to be able to depend on their **suppliers**. E.g. if a store always has items in stock then customers are more likely to shop there, even if the products are more expensive. A **reliable** business can often **charge more** for its goods and services.

Added Value is a key Operational Objective for any Business

Businesses transform **raw materials** into **finished products** to sell. **Adding value** means increasing the **difference** between the **cost** of the raw materials and the **price** that the customer pays. Adding **value** will usually increase **profits**.

> **ADDED VALUE = SALES REVENUE – COST OF BOUGHT-IN GOODS AND SERVICES**

Added value can be achieved by either **increasing** the **selling price** of the product or by **reducing** the **costs** of the raw materials. Customers will pay more for a **better quality** product, but there are other ways to increase the **value** of a product — e.g. if a business is **environmentally friendly**, offers a **quick speed of response** and is **dependable** then it can justify charging a higher selling price than its competitors.

Operational Objectives

Operational Objectives are influenced by Internal and External Factors

INTERNAL

- **Nature of the Product**: a computer technology firm is likely to have very different targets to a family-run bed and breakfast. The **computer technology company** is likely to focus on **innovation** whereas the **B&B** may be trying to increase its **capacity utilisation** by having lots of rooms full.
- **Availability of Resources**: many businesses would like to **increase output** but are limited by whether they have enough **resources**. For example, it won't be possible to produce 500 hand-painted dolls' houses in 3 days if the company only employs five carpenters.
- **Other departments**: objectives and decisions made in the **finance**, **marketing** and **HR** departments will affect what the production department can actually achieve, and vice-versa.
- **Overall objectives**: for example, if a business is concerned about its **environmental impact**, the production process will have to be more environmentally friendly.

EXTERNAL

- **Competitors' Performance**: many firms set targets in **reaction** to their **rivals' actions**. For example, if a rival gains market share, you would also probably try to increase your share of the market to make sure they don't overtake you (or leave you even further behind). **Competition** from **abroad**, e.g. China, is forcing companies to set stricter **cost** and **efficiency** objectives.
- **Market conditions**: e.g. if customers are spending less money in a **particular market**, or if there are **more competitors** in a market, this can affect any operational objectives.
- **Demand for Product**: businesses should try to make sure that **output** is not higher than **demand**, so they might set an objective to increase **flexibility** of production (see p.54).
- **Changing Customer Needs**: e.g. if customers indicate that they'd like a firm to behave more **ethically** this can affect **costs** and **environmental** objectives.
- **New technology**: the production process often needs to **adapt** to make the most of new technology.

Operational Objectives can affect the Method of Production

There are **five common methods** of production:

Job production	Production of **one-off items** by **skilled workers**.
Flow production	Mass production on a **continuous production line** with **division of labour**.
Batch production	Production of **small batches** of **identical items**.
Cell production	Production divided into **sets of tasks**, each set completed by a **work group**.
Lean production	Streamlined production with **waste at a minimum**.

1) A business that is trying to improve the **quality** of its goods might use **job** or **cell** production.
2) **Batch** or **flow** production methods could be used by a business trying to achieve **efficiency**, **dependability** and **speed of response** objectives.
3) **Lean production** could help to meet **environmental** and **efficiency** objectives whilst ensuring high **quality**.

Practice Questions

Q1 Identify eight types of operational objective.
Q2 How could a company increase the added value of one of its products?
Q3 Name two different internal factors that could influence operational objectives.

Exam Questions

Q1 Explain how external factors influence the operational objectives of a business. [6 marks]

Q2 Analyse the effects on the operational objectives of a global coffee shop chain if the price of coffee beans increases rapidly. [9 marks]

Increase the flexibility of your workforce through daily yoga sessions...

What do you mean it's not that kind of flexibility? Anyway, make sure you learn the different operational objectives and the internal and external factors that can influence them. Don't forget those production methods either...

Capacity Utilisation

Businesses need to analyse capacity utilisation data before making important operational decisions...

Capacity is Maximum Output with the Resources Currently Available

1) The **capacity** of an organisation is the **maximum** output that it can produce in a given period without buying any more fixed assets — machinery, factory space, etc.

2) Capacity depends on the **number of employees** and how skilled they are.

3) It also depends on the **technology** the business has — what **machinery** it has, what state it's in, what kind of computer system it has, etc.

4) The kind of **production process** the business uses will also affect its capacity.

5) The amount of **investment** in the business is also a factor.

Check out the capacity on that...

Capacity utilisation is how much **capacity** a business is **using**. The following formula can be used to calculate it:

$$\text{Capacity Utilisation (\%)} = \frac{\text{Output}}{\text{Capacity}} \times 100$$

Examples: a hotel with half its rooms booked out has a **capacity utilisation** of **50%**.
A clothing factory with an output of 70 000 shirts per month and a capacity of 100 000 shirts per month is running at **70% capacity utilisation**.

90% Capacity Utilisation is better than 100% Capacity Utilisation

High capacity utilisation is better than low capacity utilisation. However, **100% capacity utilisation** has drawbacks:

1) Businesses have to consider all their **operational objectives** when they plan their capacity usage. **Cost** isn't the only thing to think about — it might not be possible to operate at 100% capacity and keep **quality** levels high.

2) The business may have to **turn away** potential **customers** because it can't increase output any more.

3) There's no **downtime** — machines are on **all the time**. If a machine **breaks down**, it'll cause **delays** as work piles up **waiting** for it to be fixed. There's no time for equipment **maintenance**, which can reduce the life of machinery.

4) There's no **margin of error**. Everything has to be perfect first time, which causes **stress** to managers. **Mistakes** are more likely when everyone's working flat out.

5) The business can't **temporarily increase output** for seasonal demand or one-off orders.

6) If output is greater than demand, there'll be **surplus stock** hanging about waiting to be sold. It's not good to have valuable **working capital** (see p.72) tied up in stock.

Businesses should plan production levels to achieve <u>almost</u> full capacity utilisation.

Firms with High Capacity Utilisation can Increase their Capacity

Firms that are operating at close to 100% capacity utilisation don't just stop accepting new orders. They have ways of **increasing** their **capacity** so that they can **match** their **output** to **demand**. The best way to do this depends on whether the rise in demand is expected to be **temporary** or **long-term**.

1) Businesses can **increase capacity** by using their facilities for **more** of the **working week**. They can have staff working in two or three **shifts** in a day, and on weekends and bank holidays.

2) Businesses can buy **more machines**, if they can afford them (and the staff needed to operate them).

3) Businesses can **increase** their **staff levels** in the long run by recruiting new permanent staff. In the short run they can employ **temporary staff**, **part-time staff**, or get their staff to work **overtime**.

4) Businesses can also increase their capacity by increasing **productivity**. They can reorganise production by reallocating staff to the busiest areas, and they can increase employee **motivation**.

5) If the rise in demand is **temporary** then businesses might choose to **subcontract** work:

- **Subcontracting** (or **outsourcing**) is when a business uses another firm to do some work on its behalf. E.g. a manufacturer of detergent might make detergent for a **supermarket** and package it with the supermarket's own label.

- Companies can **subcontract** work to other businesses in **busy periods**. This means they can meet **unexpected increases in demand** without increasing their own capacity and having the costs of extra staff and facilities all year round.

Capacity Utilisation

Under-Utilisation is Inefficient and increases Unit Costs

Low capacity utilisation is called **under-utilisation**. It's **inefficient** because it means a business is **not** getting **use** out of **machines** and **facilities** that have been paid for.

1) Under-utilisation increases costs because it causes **fixed costs** to be spread over **fewer units of output**, so **unit costs increase**.

2) Higher capacity utilisation means an increase in the number of units output **without** increasing the **fixed costs**. So the **total costs** are spread over **more units**.

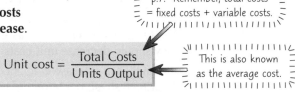

For more on unit costs, see p.7. Remember, total costs = fixed costs + variable costs.

$$\text{Unit cost} = \frac{\text{Total Costs}}{\text{Units Output}}$$

This is also known as the average cost.

Example: A chocolate factory's total costs are **£7200** a month. In November, the factory output **18 000** chocolate bars, giving a unit cost of **£0.40**. In December, staff holidays caused output to fall to **16 000 bars**, meaning that the unit cost rose to **£0.45**.

Firms deal with Under-Utilisation in Two ways

Sometimes firms have **too much capacity** and **not enough demand** for their product, which leads to **under-utilisation**. When this happens, they'll **first** try to **increase demand**, but if that doesn't work, they need to **reduce capacity**.

1) Businesses stimulate demand by changing the **marketing mix** (see p.40-41). E.g. they can change the **promotion** of a product, or change its **price** or its **distribution**.

2) Businesses can also fill spare capacity by **subcontracting** work for other firms. It's often better to make goods for a **competitor** and make a bit of money than it is to leave **machinery** sitting around doing **nothing**.

3) If a business can't increase demand for their product, they need to **reduce their capacity** by closing part of their production facilities. This is called **rationalisation** (or **downsizing**).

4) Businesses can reduce capacity in the **short term** by stopping **overtime** or reducing the length of the working week, allocating staff to **other work** in the business, and by not renewing **temporary contracts**.

5) Businesses can reduce capacity in the **long term** by not **replacing** staff as they retire (natural wastage), making staff **redundant**, and by **selling off** factories or equipment.

Firms have to consider how their Capacity Needs will Change over Time

1) Demand **changes** over time, so firms must think about demand in the **future** as well as the current demand.

2) The key to **long-term** success is planning **capacity** changes to match long-term changes in demand. You can use **market research** to help **predict** future demand, but it's not 100% certain. There's always an element of **risk**.

3) **Short-term** changes in **capacity utilisation** provide **flexibility**. Firms should be flexible and **temporarily** increase existing capacity utilisation if an increase in demand isn't expected to continue **long-term** — e.g with seasonal goods like Christmas crackers, goods heading towards decline in their life cycle, and one-off special orders.

4) **Long-term** solutions end up giving **lower unit costs** — as long as **predictions** of demand turn out to be **true**.

Practice Questions

Q1 Calculate capacity utilisation for a restaurant that has 64 seats but only 44 people dining each night.

Q2 Give five ways in which a firm can increase its capacity.

Q3 Calculate the unit cost of one shirt, if a factory makes 450 shirts a month and has total monthly costs of £1719.

Answers on p.106.

Exam Question

Q1 A cinema is open 7 days a week. It only has one screen, with 300 seats, and shows 3 films a day. The cinema gets 2205 customers per week.
a) Calculate the cinema's capacity utilisation. [3 marks]
b) Use your calculation to advise the cinema on its plans for the future. [6 marks]

She cannae take any more, Jim...

Businesses need to keep an eye on capacity utilisation. Under-utilisation is a consequence of low demand. When a business launches a product, capacity utilisation often starts out low and then builds up as demand for the new product increases. It really is worth your while knowing how businesses should deal with high and low capacity utilisation.

Increasing Efficiency and Productivity

The more efficient you are at revision, the quicker this page will all be over.

Productivity and Efficiency are Not the Same Thing

1) **Productivity** is measured as the **output per worker** in a given time period.

2) **Efficiency** is all about getting **more output** from a given amount of inputs. Being efficient just means **reducing the waste** of all the inputs, e.g. time and materials. Greater efficiency should **decrease unit costs** and **increase profits**.

3) Increasing productivity can increase efficiency, but this **isn't** necessarily the case. E.g. a farmer shearing 8 sheep per hour and getting all the wool is **less productive** but **more efficient** than a farmer shearing 20 sheep per hour but wasting half the wool.

Dave's productivity currently stood at 900 rabbits per hour.

Labour Productivity measures How Much each Employee Produces

Companies need to know how productive their workforce is, because changes in labour productivity can have a massive impact on the business. This is especially true in **labour-intensive** firms, where labour costs are a high proportion of total costs.

$$\text{Labour Productivity} = \frac{\text{Output per period}}{\text{Number of employees}}$$

> **Example**: A factory employs 90 workers to produce 9000 DVD players per week.
> **Labour Productivity** = 9000 ÷ 90 workers = **100** DVD players per worker per week.

1) The **higher** the labour productivity, the **better** the workforce is performing. As labour productivity **increases**, labour costs per unit **fall** (see p.84).

2) If labour productivity is **low**, managers will try to increase it (see below).

Increasing Labour Productivity influences Efficiency

Increasing productivity can **improve** the efficiency of a business. If the **same number of workers** are producing **more units of output** in the **same amount of time** then unit costs will be lower.

Ways to increase labour productivity

- Labour productivity can be improved by **improving worker motivation** (see p.90-91).
- **Training** can make workers more productive.
- **New technology** can increase the speed at which workers can do their job.

However, **increasing productivity** is not always a good thing for the business or for the workers.

1) Encouraging workers to produce more by offering **bonuses** and **incentives** for increased output could mean that the **quality suffers** or that **more waste** is produced.

2) If the business is not planning to **increase its capacity**, then training workers to be more productive could result in **redundancies** and **job losses** — this will **lower morale** amongst staff.

3) New technology can be very **expensive** and businesses need to decide whether it's worth **investing** in new machines and software.

> - Businesses will base their **decisions** about labour productivity on the **value added** and **efficiency**.
> - If labour costs only make up a **small percentage** of the **production costs** then it may not be worth investing lots of time and effort into increasing labour productivity.
> - Increasing productivity could lead to **more waste** of raw materials which could reduce value added and will have a negative impact on the environment.

Lean Production Methods aim to Increase Efficiency

Lean production isn't a good thing for everyone — it can mean that jobs are lost as efficiency increases.

1) **Lean production** is an **efficient** form of production that keeps **waste** (of time and resources) to a **minimum**.

2) **Inefficient** production methods increase **costs**, so **lean** production can **save** businesses a lot of money.

3) Businesses can use lean production to help them meet some of their **operational objectives** (see p.54). E.g. reducing waste will have a **positive impact** on **costs**, **value added** and the **environment**.

4) **Lean** production methods include **just-in-time**, **time-based management** (see next page) and **kaizen** (see p.63).

Increasing Efficiency and Productivity

Just-In-Time (JIT) Production keeps stock levels *Very Low*

1) **Just-in-time** production aims to **reduce** waste of materials and products by having as **little stock** as possible. Ideally, all raw materials come in one door, are made into products and go straight out another door — all **just in time** for delivery to customers.

2) JIT is based on very efficient **stock control** (see p.64). **Kanban** is the JIT system of triggering **repeat orders**. When staff reach coloured kanban cards towards the end of a batch of components, they order more straight away. The **supply** of components is **linked directly** to the **demand** for components, and there's no need for lots of stock.

3) JIT has **advantages** — **storage costs** are reduced and **cash flow** is improved as money isn't tied up in stock. There's **less waste** because there's less out-of-date or damaged stock lying around. The business is more **flexible** so it can cope with changes in **demand** and easily **adapt its products** to suit changing customer requirements.

4) There are **disadvantages** — no stock means customers can't be supplied during **production strikes**. Suppliers have to be **reliable** because there isn't much stock of raw materials to keep production going.

Time-Based Management means companies have to be *Flexible*

1) The time-based management approach aims to **reduce wasted time** in the production process.

2) Time-based management means that as well as competing on price and quality, companies can also **compete** on **time** by trying to be the **fastest** to get their product on the market. It's often used to produce **technological** items and **high fashion** clothes — areas where consumer needs change fast.

3) Time-based management depends on **flexible production facilities**, e.g. a fashion retailer might need a machine that can sew buttons onto coats one week and attach zips the next.

4) **Effective communication** between managers and production staff is essential, so the business needs to have a culture of **trust**. Staff also need to be **multi-skilled** — so **training** is important.

Advantages of Time-Based Management

- It **reduces lead times** — the time between a customer placing an order and taking delivery. So the cost of holding stock falls (see p.64).
- Reduced lead times also mean that **customer needs** can be satisfied **quicker**, giving the company a **competitive advantage**.
- **Machinery** with more than one function makes it possible to offer a more **varied** product range.
- It can help to **drive innovation** by decreasing research and development time.

5) However, some people have **criticised** time-based management for placing speed above **quality** — customers get a product sooner, but it might be faulty or not last as long.

Practice Questions

Q1 A council employs 4 workers to cut grass. They each work 35 hours per week. In total they cut 168 000 m² of grass each week. What is the labour productivity of the workers?

   A   42 000 m² per worker per hour   B   4800 m² per worker per hour
   C   1200 m² per worker per hour   D   6000 m² per worker per hour

Answer on p.107.

Q2 Give three ways a company can increase its labour productivity.

Q3 What is lean production?

Q4 Give two advantages of just-in-time production.

Exam Questions

Q1 A guitar manufacturer wants to lower the price of its guitars but wants to ensure that the value added remains the same. Analyse how efficiency and productivity could be improved to meet these goals.   **[9 marks]**

Q2 To what extent do you agree that all firms should use lean production methods?   **[12 marks]**

Just-in-time production is a good idea — just-in-time revision isn't...

Hopefully you're reading this a good few weeks before the exam and you've got time to read and scribble until it's properly embedded in your memory. If you are tight for time though, don't panic. Just do as much as you can.

Increasing Efficiency and Productivity

Most modern businesses rely heavily on technology, from automated production lines to computer systems. Technology can make a firm more cost-effective and efficient, but it needs constant updating and maintenance.

Businesses use **Two** main types of **Technology**

The main technologies that companies use in day-to-day operations are:

1) **Robotic Engineering** — using robots as part of the manufacturing process.
2) **Computer Technology** — computers are used by businesses in lots of different ways.
   Product development, business communications and finance departments all depend heavily on IT systems.

Using **Robots** can **Reduce Staffing Costs**

1) **Robots** are mostly used to replace human staff for **tasks** which are **dangerous**, **repetitive** or **boring**.

2) **Factories** and **production plants** often use **automated pickers** to take goods from the production line and pack them into boxes. It's usually **cheaper** and **faster** for robots to do this job instead of humans.

3) Companies that are planning to replace human workers with robots need to weigh up the **advantages** of using robots against the **demotivating effect** that it is likely to have on staff.

Developments in **IT** can make **Companies** more **Efficient**

1) **Computer-aided design** (CAD) uses computers to design new products, or make alterations to existing products. CAD produces 3D mock-ups on screen — this can also be useful for marketing things like new kitchens.

2) **Computer-aided manufacturing** (CAM) uses computers to produce a product, usually involving **robots** or 'computer-numerically controlled' (CNC) machines. CAM is often combined with the CAD process — products are digitally designed, and the design data fed straight into the production machine. This is called **CAD/CAM**.

3) **3D printing** can be used to produce a **prototype** from a CAD. This is a lot **cheaper** than the CAD/CAM process as you don't need to build robots to make a single item.

4) Computers make **stock control** easier. Holding stock information in a database makes it much easier to monitor when you need to order new stock. In retail, **Electronic Point of Sale (EPOS)** systems rely on barcodes to record which products are being purchased, which means stock can be re-ordered automatically. **Electronic data interchange** can be used to automatically share sales information with a supplier — having a good stock control system makes it easier for companies to move to a **just-in-time** supply system (see p.59).

5) **Spreadsheets** are very useful in marketing and finance departments. E.g. in marketing they can calculate the impact of **potential changes** in expenditure or sales, which makes **decision-making** easier.

6) **Email** is a fast and efficient method of **communicating**, both internally and externally. E.g. companies can advertise cheaply to a **target audience** of their previous customers through email.

7) The **internet** allows businesses to reach a **huge customer base**, and do business **24 hours a day**, all over the world. Customers can order products using a business's **website** rather than phoning or posting an order.

Firms need to consider the **Advantages** and **Disadvantages** of **Technology**

Most companies invest a lot of money in technology. Technology is beneficial if it leads to:

1) **Increased productivity** and **quality** — machines are often quicker and more accurate than humans.
2) **Reduced waste** through more effective production methods.
3) More **effective** and **efficient delivery** of goods and services to the customer.
4) More **effective marketing** campaigns that target the right customers.
5) **Reduced** administrative and financial **costs**.
6) **Better communications** both internally and externally.

However, introducing new technology or updating older systems can create problems:

1) **Initial costs** of technology may be **high**.
2) Technology requires **maintenance** and **constant updating** in order to stay current, which can also be **expensive**.
3) New IT systems may create an **increased** need for **staff training**.
4) Some technologies might replace manual work, leading to **staff redundancies**.

Increasing Efficiency and Productivity

A *Capital-Intensive* firm has **Lots** of **Machinery**

1) A **capital-intensive** business uses more **machinery** and relatively few **workers**.

2) **Larger** firms tend to be more **capital-intensive** than smaller companies. E.g. the Morgan Motor Company makes a small number of hand-built sports cars using lots of **labour**, whereas BMW uses more **robots** and machinery.

3) A rise in the **cost** of **labour** can also cause companies to **switch** to a **capital-intensive** method of production.

Advantages of Capital-Intensive Production	Disadvantages of Capital-Intensive Production
• **Cheaper** than manual labour in the **long term**. • Machinery is often **more precise** than human workers, which might lead to more **consistent quality** levels. • Machinery is able to work **24/7**. • Machines are **easier** to **manage** than people.	• High **set-up** costs. • Machines are usually only suited to one task, which makes them **inflexible**. • If machinery **breaks down**, it can lead to long **delays**. • The fear of being replaced by a machine can cause workers' **motivation** to **decrease**.

A *Labour-Intensive* firm is very *People-Heavy*

1) A **labour-intensive** firm uses more **workers** and less **machinery**. For example, the **NHS** is very labour-intensive.

2) In countries where labour is relatively **cheap** (e.g. China), **labour-intensive** methods of production are common.

Advantages of Labour-Intensive Production	Disadvantages of Labour-Intensive Production
• People are **flexible** and can be **retrained**. • **Cheaper** for **small-scale** production. • Labour-intensive methods are also **cheaper** where **low-cost labour** is available, e.g. China and India. • Workers can **solve** any **problems** that arise during production and suggest ways to **improve quality**.	• It's **harder** to **manage** people than machines. • People can be **unreliable** — they can get sick. • People can't work without **breaks** or **holidays**. • **Wage increases** mean that the cost of labour can increase over time. • Labour costs as a % of turnover (p.84) are **high**.

Businesses need to have the *Right Mix* of *People, Machines* and *Materials*

1) Businesses should try to **optimise resources** (**materials**, **machinery** and **people**) in order to meet objectives. How hard it is to get this right depends on the **complexity** of the product and the number of **production stages**. A business needs to strike the right **balance** between **labour-** and **capital-intensity** at each stage of production.

2) The **design** of the product affects the mix — e.g. freshly squeezed orange juice has just one component (oranges), but a car has hundreds. The **higher** the number of **components**, the more **complicated** the product is to produce, so the **harder** it is to get the correct mix of people, machines and materials.

3) Businesses can have problems getting the right mix if there's a **shortage** of suitably skilled **labour**. E.g. at the moment there's a very limited supply of **nurses**, **geologists** and **civil engineers** in the UK.

4) Businesses are also limited by their **finances**. Most companies would have the **latest technology** if they could **afford** it, but in reality **smaller firms** can rarely afford to keep updating their machinery.

Practice Questions

Q1 What is meant by CAD? How can a business use it?

Q2 Give three advantages and three disadvantages of using technology in business.

Q3 Give three benefits of capital-intensive production and three drawbacks of labour-intensive production.

Exam Questions

Q1 Plastoise is a plaster ornament manufacturer that specialises in making plaster animals. Analyse how they could use technology to develop, design and make new products. [9 marks]

Q2 A plumbing supplies manufacturer is changing its production system to be more capital-intensive. Evaluate the effects that this will have on the business, the employees and the customers. [16 marks]

If these pages are repetitive and boring — they're the work of a robot...

Reading through this lot is enough to make you wonder how big businesses ever coped before technology came along. Robots might be cheaper than humans, but they tell lousy jokes, don't flirt, and are no good at making tea...

Improving Quality

Increased competition means that firms now compete through quality as well as price.
High quality can increase revenue and reduce costs.

A **High Quality Product** can **Increase Profits** but may have **Drawbacks**

1) It's **important** that companies produce **quality** goods — poor quality leads to
   customer dissatisfaction and a **bad reputation** for the business.

2) Most **customers** realise that **lower priced** goods won't be as **high** quality as more **expensive** ones,
   but they do expect a product to be **fit for purpose** (to do the job it's intended for).

3) Producing high quality products allows for **premium pricing** and
   gives workers pride in their work, which can increase **morale** and **motivation**.

4) It also allows the business to **reduce its costs** and **increase its revenue**:

   - Less **raw materials** and less **worker** and **machinery** time get used up by **mistakes**.
   - You don't need as much **advertising** and **promotional** material to persuade **shops** to stock high quality goods.
   - There are **fewer complaints** and **refunds** so employees can spend their time on other things.
   - You don't need to **discount** prices to sell **damaged stock**.
   - Quality can function as a **unique selling point (USP)** for your product.
   - High quality products improve the **image** and **reputation** of the business.
   - Quality goods and services make it easy to keep **existing customers** and **attract new customers**.

5) However, it can be **difficult** for companies to improve the quality of their products **efficiently**.

6) There is a **limit** to how much quality can be improved — workers have to know when the quality
   is **good enough**. Trying to make every single product 100% perfect could prove **costly** to the business.

7) If a company **outsources** some of its work it can be difficult to make sure
   the outsourced work is of the **same quality** that is expected within the business.

Quality Control and Quality Assurance are Different Things

There are **two main** ways for a company to **check** it's producing goods of a suitable quality:

1) **Quality control** means **checking goods** as you make them or when they arrive from suppliers
   to see if anything is wrong with them. It's often done by specially trained **quality inspectors**.

2) **Quality assurance** means introducing measures into the **production process** to try to ensure
   things don't go **wrong** in the first place. It assumes you can **prevent errors** from being made
   in the first place, rather than **eliminating faulty goods** once they've been made.

Quality Control (QC)	Quality Assurance (QA)
• Assumes that errors are **unavoidable**. • **Detects** errors and puts them **right**. • Quality control **inspectors** check other people's work, and are **responsible** for quality.	• Assumes that errors are **avoidable**. • **Prevents** errors and aims to get it right **first time**. • Employees **check** their own work. Workers are responsible for passing on **good quality** work to the next stage of the production process.

Quality Assurance can be more Motivating than Quality Control

1) **Quality assurance** is a more modern approach to quality control.

2) Under a self-checking system, it's **everyone's responsibility** to produce good work. Everyone should try
   to get it **right first time**. Workers can **reject** components or work in progress if they're not up to standard.
   They don't pass the poor quality off as **someone else's problem**.

3) **Empowering** employees to **self-check** the quality of their work can be highly **motivating**.

4) **Training** is important for quality assurance. Workers have to be trained to produce good quality products and
   services. New recruits get this as part of their **induction**. Experienced workers might need to be **retrained**.

5) Workers must be **motivated** and **committed** to quality for quality assurance schemes to work.

6) The ultimate aim of quality assurance is to create a culture of **zero defects**.

7) Both methods have their **drawbacks** — unless **all products** are tested during quality control, some **faulty** products
   will slip through. Quality assurance can result in products only being '**acceptable**', not of a **high standard**.

Improving Quality

Total Quality Management assures Commitment To Quality

1) **Total Quality Management** (TQM) means the **whole workforce** is committed to quality improvements. The idea is that **every department** focuses on quality in order to improve the **overall quality** of the products and services.

2) With TQM, every employee has to try to **satisfy customers** and **co-workers** — customers need to be happy with products or services they are being sold, and co-workers need to be happy with work you are passing on to them.

Advantages of TQM	Disadvantages of TQM
• Because all employees are involved with improving quality, TQM can help them to bond as a **team**. • TQM boosts a company's **reputation** for providing quality services or products. • TQM usually leads to fewer **faulty** products being made — so the business creates less **waste**.	• It can take a **long time** to introduce TQM. Companies might not see immediate improvements in quality. • TQM can **demotivate staff** — it can seem like a lot of effort to think about quality in all parts of the business. • TQM is usually **expensive** to introduce — it often means investing in **training** for all employees.

Businesses may use Other Methods to Improve Quality

Quality Circles

1) **Quality circles** meet at regular intervals to discuss quality control issues.
2) They use the knowledge of employees from **various departments** and **all levels** of the organisation.
3) Quality circles aim to **identify** and **solve** specific quality problems that arise.
4) They are a great way to get staff **involved** and can lead to increased **motivation** and **productivity**.
5) However, suggestions can often be **unrealistic** and management may **not listen** to the floor staff.

Kaizen

1) The **kaizen** approach is a **lean production method** (see p.58-59) that means that employees should be **improving** their work slightly **all the time**, instead of just making one-off improvements.
2) Employees are **encouraged** to question **why** a problem has occurred.
3) Employees at the bottom of the hierarchy have to be given some control over **decision-making**.
4) **Kaizen** helps workers feel involved in **quality assurance**. It's also **cheap** to introduce.
5) The downside of **kaizen** is that, because it makes **small changes** over time, it's not great for businesses that **urgently** need to improve quality. It needs the firm to be willing to commit to the method in the **long term**.

Practice Questions

Q1 Give two reasons why high quality reduces costs.
Q2 What's the difference between quality control and quality assurance?
Q3 Describe two advantages and two disadvantages of TQM.
Q4 What are 'quality circles'?

Staff adopted a new quality assurance method — if they didn't turn up to work, nothing couldn't go wrong...

Exam Questions

Q1 The Managing Director of Ropey Textiles decides to introduce further quality control into the production process. Explain why employees may be resistant to quality control. [6 marks]

Q2 Lightoptic manufacture table lamps. Recently a large number of customers have been complaining about the quality of the lamps. Analyse how Lightoptic could ensure its lamps are high quality. [9 marks]

Examiners — the ultimate quality control inspectors...

Poor quality products can have huge impacts on a business. They can lead to decreased sales, a poor reputation, waste or discounted goods, complaints, and additional costs in bringing them up to scratch. Companies like to get it right first time — just like in your exam really, get it spot on first time and bathe in the glory of your achievements.

Managing Inventory

Managing inventory is a fancy name for keeping track of stock levels.

It's **Costly** to hold lots of **Stock**

1) A business's **stock** includes the **raw materials** needed for making a product, the materials that are currently being used for **products-in-progress** and the store of **finished goods** that a firm holds to supply to customers. These days, firms don't tend to hold much stock — because of the **costs** involved.

2) **Storage costs** are the most **obvious cost** of holding stock. Storage costs include **rent** for the warehouse and also the non-obvious costs of **heating, lighting, refrigeration, security** etc.

3) **Wastage costs** are the costs of **throwing away** useless stock. The longer a business holds stock, the more likely it is to create waste. Stock gets **physically damaged** as time goes on, and can also go **out of fashion**.

4) The **opportunity cost** (see p.21) is the cost of **investing** money in stock instead of **something else**. Capital tied up in stock is **unproductive** and could be used more productively elsewhere.

Stock Control aims to keep levels of stock **Just Right**

1) Most businesses try to **minimise** the level of stock they're holding. The **maximum** level of stock a business wants to hold depends on the size of their warehouses, their production method (see p.55) and on **opportunity cost**.

2) Businesses that use **flow production** need a **large stock** of **raw materials**, whereas **batch production** leads to large stocks of **work-in-progress**. **Job production** often means there is **no stock** of **finished goods** to be stored and **cell production** usually relies on **just-in-time** stock control (see p.59).

3) A business needs a **minimum** level of stock so that it **won't run out** of raw materials or finished goods. This minimum stock level is called **buffer stock**.

4) The **amount** of **buffer stock** needed depends on the storage **space** available, the kind of product (**perishable**, or something that keeps), the **rate** at which stocks are used up, and the **lead time**.

5) The **lead time** is the time it takes for goods to **arrive** after ordering them from the supplier. The **longer** the lead time, the **more buffer stocks** you need to hold — if customer demand suddenly went up, you wouldn't want to wait a long time for stocks to arrive from the supplier.

6) The **re-order quantity** is the amount the company orders from its supplier. The stock level at which this re-order is placed is called the **re-order level** and is calculated using:

   If lead time is in weeks, use the average weekly usage.

   > **Re-order level = lead time (in days) × average daily usage + buffer stock level**

7) **Inventory control charts** allow managers to **analyse** and **control** stock over a period of time — as shown below.

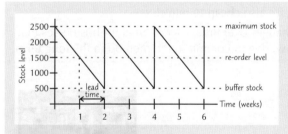

1) The **buffer stock level** is **500 units**. The **lead time** is **1 week**, and the business uses **1000 units** a week. That means they have to **re-order** stock when they have: 1 × 1000 + 500 = **1500** units left (so they don't go below their buffer stock level). 1500 units is the **re-order level**.

2) The **re-order quantity** is **2000 units**. This takes them back to their **maximum stock level** of 2500 units.

Practice Questions

Q1 Name three costs involved in holding stock.

Q2 In inventory control, what is the lead time?

Q3 Find the re-order level if lead time is 5 days, daily usage is 9 units and 7 units of buffer stock are required.

Exam Question

Answers on p.107.

Q1 A bakery monitors its stock levels of flour over a 10 day period. They started with 70 bags of flour, they use 20 bags per day and keep a stock buffer of 10 bags. Each time they place an order it takes 2 days to arrive and they order 60 bags each time. Draw a stock control chart to show the bakery's stock of flour. [4 marks]

It's time to sit back and take stock of what you've learnt...

Make sure you know and can read off all the different parts of an inventory control chart. You'll also need to know all the definitions on this page and how to calculate re-order level. This revision lark is a piece of cake, isn't it?

Managing Supply Chains

Every business in the supply chain needs to pull their weight, or production just doesn't happen...

Businesses need to have **Flexible** and **Dependable Supply Chains**

1) A **supply chain** consists of the **group** of firms that are involved in **all** the various **processes** required to make a **finished product** or **service** available to the customer.

2) The chain **begins** with the provider of **raw materials** and **ends** with the firm that sells the **finished product**.

3) The members of a supply chain will **vary** depending on the type of product or service, but will typically include **suppliers**, **manufacturers**, **distributors** and **retailers**.

4) **All** the **members** of the supply chain need to be **dependable**. If any of them are **unreliable**, the product won't be on the shelves when it needs to be, or the **quality** will be **poor**, which reflects **badly** on the company selling it.

5) Businesses need to be **flexible** on the **time taken** to supply goods and the **volume** of goods they supply. They can utilise a **flexible workforce** or use **outsourcing** (see below) to help manage sudden **changes in demand**.

6) A supplier that can offer **faster response** times than its competitors is more likely to gain the contract. This might be achieved through maintaining a **range of delivery** contracts to suit a business's needs.

"We should be able to get those components to you by 1952."

Businesses need to match **Supply** to **Demand**

Peripheral workers can help deal with changes in demand

1) **Core workers** are employees who are **essential** to a business, like senior managers and skilled workers. They are employed on **full-time**, **permanent** contracts. They are the workers that the company couldn't function effectively without, even if demand is low.

2) **Peripheral workers** are employees who **aren't essential** to a business, but that the business employs when they need **more staff**. Businesses keep their **fixed costs down** by employing peripheral workers on **temporary**, **part-time** or **zero-hours** contracts.

3) Peripheral workers can help a business deal with unforeseen or foreseen **increases in demand**. E.g. a supermarket might employ seasonal workers in order to deal with greater demand at Christmas time.

Outsourcing can help a business to meet demand

1) **Outsourcing** (or **subcontracting**) is when businesses **contract out** some activities to other businesses rather than doing them **in-house**.

2) Businesses can outsource some or all of the **product manufacturing** to deal with **increased demand**. They might also outsource things like **finance**, **recruitment**, **advertising** and **IT** — things that the business doesn't **specialise** in but sometimes needs.

3) Outsourcing can **benefit** businesses because they might be able to **accept contracts** which they would otherwise have turned down. They can also benefit from the **specialised knowledge** of the businesses they outsource to. Outsourcing also means that the business doesn't have to pay for permanent staff when they're only needed occasionally, so it **reduces costs**.

4) The main **disadvantage** of outsourcing is that the business doesn't have **control** over the **quality** of the outsourced work — if the work is bad, it can have a **negative effect** on the business's reputation.

Mass customisation allows businesses to supply tailor-made products

1) **Mass customisation** is a method of **producing to order** (products are made **after** the order is placed). It combines the **flexibility** of a custom-made product with the low cost of **mass production**.

2) A business that develops its capacity for mass customisation must have a **flexible** and **efficient production process** and **supply chain**.

3) It allows for an **increase in customer choice** without a corresponding increase in costs and it can lead to a **competitive advantage**.

4) However, it can be **very difficult** for a business to make mass customisation **efficient** and **profitable**. Customised products can be **expensive** and it can take a **long time** for them to be delivered to customers — this is acceptable for **luxury items** but not for everyday things.

Managing Supply Chains

Companies need to Choose their Suppliers Carefully

The most **effective suppliers** are those who offer products or services that **match** (or **exceed**) the **needs** of your business. So when you are looking for **suppliers**, it's best to be **sure** of your **business needs** and what you want to achieve. The most important factors to consider are:

Price	The **total cost** of acquiring the product. Firms have to decide **how much** they are willing to pay and whether **cost** is their **first priority**. If they want to cut down the time it takes to serve customers, suppliers that offer faster delivery will rate higher than those that compete on price alone. The **cheaper** a supplier is, the more **value added** to the final product. However, the **cheapest** supplier isn't always the **best** as they will often supply **lower quality** products.
Payment Terms	Companies need to know **how much** they need to pay, **how** it has to be paid and **when** it should be paid by. **New companies** will often have to pay for all the goods **up front**, whereas companies with a **well-established relationship** with their supplier will be given **credit**, which **delays** the payment for a certain amount of **time** (often 30 days).
Quality	The **quality** of supplies needs to be **consistent**. In recent years, customers have become much **more selective** about the quality of the product. Customers will associate **poor quality** with the business they buy from, not their suppliers.
Capacity	Businesses need to select **suppliers** who are able to **meet** any **peaks** in **demand** for particular products / services. Big businesses usually opt to buy in bulk in hope of getting a **discount**.
Reliability	If **a supplier** lets a **firm** down, that firm may not be able to supply its **own** customers. Suppliers need to **deliver high-quality products on time**, or give plenty of **warning** if they can't.
Flexibility	**Suppliers** need to be able to **respond easily** to **changes** in a company's **requirements**. Efficient production relies on suppliers who can provide extra (or fewer) supplies at **short notice**. Flexible suppliers will also be willing to adapt to meet the company's other requirements — such as becoming more **environmentally-friendly**.

Companies build Relationships with their Suppliers

A **strategic working relationship** is one where both companies in the relationship can get **long-term benefits** from **working together**. There are several ways for companies to build strategic working relationships with their suppliers:

Mr MacDonald and Mr Paulin had spent three days choosing a supplier for a new stapler.

1) **Linked Networks** — **shared IT systems** such as **inventory (stock) control management** and **electronic data interchange** allow both the company and its supplier to view stock levels, so they both know in plenty of time when more supplies will be needed. This can improve **efficiency**, cut **costs**, and improve **customer value**.

2) **JIT (Just-in-Time) Systems** (see p.59) — these are becoming a popular way of managing operations. The goal of JIT systems is to have only the **right amounts** of **materials** arrive at precisely the **times** they are **needed**. Because supplies arrive just as they are needed, you don't need a big warehouse, and there's **less waste**.

3) **Shared Costs** — if a business and its supplier are producing similar goods, there's a good chance they'll be able to save money by sharing **specialist equipment** and storing their goods in the same **warehouse**.

4) **Innovation** — companies who work **closely** with their suppliers are able to **share new ideas** and ultimately make or save **more money** through innovation. They could work together to improve the **manufacturing process**, develop a **new product** or even alter the **supply network** — all these things can help both the company and the supplier to save money.

Managing Supply Chains

A *Well-Managed Supply Chain* can *Improve Operational Performance...*

1) If a business works **closely** with the **right suppliers**, operational **performance** will improve.
2) **Productivity** will **increase**, which causes **costs** to fall (see p.58), so **profits** will increase.
3) A business with an **efficient supply chain** is in a much better position to meet its customers' **expectations**.
4) Businesses should constantly be looking to improve their **supply chain**, and they can do this in several ways:

   1) A company's buyers need to make sure that they **only buy** the **supplies** that the **company** really **needs**.

   2) They also need to understand the difference between a **strategic supplier**, who provides goods or services that are essential to the business — such as high-value raw materials, and a **non-strategic supplier** who provides low-value supplies such as office stationery. It's important to spend **more time** selecting and managing **strategic suppliers** than non-strategic suppliers.

   3) It's often easier, and generally more **cost-effective**, for businesses to **limit** the number of **sources** they buy from. However, it's **dangerous** to have just **one supplier** because if there are ever problems with that supplier, the business has nowhere to turn.

   4) It's always worth having an **alternative supply source** ready to help in difficult times. This is really important for suppliers who are essential to the success of the business.

...and efficiently *Match Supply* to *Demand*

When demand for a product **increases** the whole supply chain needs to adapt. For example:

- The **retailer** might hire more **peripheral workers** on **short-term** contracts to keep the shelves full and to deal with customers.
- The **distributor** could increase the number of deliveries by **outsourcing** some work to another distributor.
- The **manufacturer** could temporarily increase its **capacity utilisation** (see p.56) to 100% and get more raw materials from its **alternative supply sources**.
- The **supply sources** may have to be able to supply more **raw materials**.

See p.65 for more on peripheral workers and outsourcing.

Practice Questions

Q1 Give three types of company that you would expect to find as part of a supply chain.
Q2 What is mass customisation?
Q3 Give six qualities that a business would look for in a supplier.
Q4 What is the difference between a strategic supplier and a non-strategic supplier?
Q5 Why is it risky for a business to rely on a single supplier?

Exam Questions

Q1 Alpha Beefs Ltd is looking for a supplier of beef to use in its new range of beef pies. Discuss the factors it should consider before deciding which one to choose. [8 marks]

Q2 Mr Brown, director of Brown's Brushes Ltd, wants to improve his relationship with his wood supplier. Discuss the ways in which he could achieve this. [8 marks]

Q3 Gordon's Cycles is a custom-made bike manufacturer. In July, demand for their bikes increased by 50%. Analyse the short-term and long-term impacts on different parts of the supply chain. [9 marks]

Supply me to the moon, let me sing among the stock...

If you're a business, the relationship with your supplier might be the best one you'll ever have. Or the worst. If your suppliers do what they're supposed to when they're supposed to, there's a good chance that the production process will all run to plan. If they're late, or just don't deliver, production stops — which isn't an ideal situation...

Financial Objectives

Here's where the real fun starts — it's finance time.

Financial Objectives are what the business wants to Achieve Financially

1) **Financial objectives** are **financial goals** that a business wants to achieve. Businesses usually have **specific targets** in mind, and a **specific period of time** to achieve them in. E.g. a business might have an objective to increase its profits by 10% within three years.

2) The financial objectives will be set by **financial managers** and will help the business achieve its corporate objectives. They must also be **consistent** with the **functional objectives** of the other departments.

3) Financial objectives can improve **coordination** between teams, act as a **focus** for **decision-making** and allow shareholders to judge whether a business would be a worthwhile **investment**.

4) Businesses look at their **financial data** (e.g. cash flow figures and profit margins) to assess their **financial position**. They can then **set objectives** based on what they need to improve.

Companies set Revenue, Costs and Profit Objectives

For more on revenue, costs and profit, see p.6

1) **Revenue objectives** are often set to **increase** the **value** or **volume** of **sales**. Examples might be 'increase sales revenue by 5% in the next year' or 'beat a competitor's monthly sales'.

2) **Costs objectives** are usually set to **minimise costs**. Examples of costs objectives for the next year could be 'reduce costs of raw materials by 10%', or 'reduce fixed costs by 15%'. If costs are reduced and the business still sells the same number of products at the same price, this will **increase** its overall **profits**. Businesses have to be careful that cutting costs doesn't reduce the **quality** of their products or services, or raise **ethical questions** about how they operate — otherwise sales might drop and they'd end up with **lower profits** instead of higher profits.

3) **Profit objectives** might set a target figure for profit or for a percentage increase from the previous year. Since revenue, costs and profit are closely linked, achieving revenue and costs objectives can help achieve profit objectives.

Cash Flow Objectives aim to Improve Cash Flow

1) **Cash flow** is all the money flowing **into** and **out of** the business over a period of time, calculated at the exact time it **enters** or **leaves** the bank account or till. On the other hand, **profit** includes all transactions that will lead to cash in or out, now, or in the **future**.

2) Cash flow calculations are pretty much the most important thing to a business in the **short term**. Businesses need cash to survive. Looking at the **long term**, making a profit is the **main objective**.

3) If a business allows payments to be made on **credit** (see p.72), this may **damage** their cash flow. Similarly, if a business needs to spend a lot of money on a new computer system or machinery, the outflow of cash could lead the business to a potential **crisis**. If a business **produces too much**, they'll have to **pay** suppliers and staff **so much** that they'll become **insolvent** before they have the chance to **get paid** by their customers. This is called **overtrading**.

Insolvency means that a business is unable to pay its debts. If a sole trader or partnership business is insolvent, the owner may have to declare bankruptcy.

4) **Cash flow objectives** are put in place to help **prevent** cash flow problems. Businesses may set objectives to spread revenue or costs more **evenly** throughout the year, acquire a specified amount of **liquid** assets (an asset that can be turned into cash quickly) or target a **minimum cash balance**.

Return on Investment Objectives help a business stay Profitable

1) Businesses might set objectives for **return on investment** (**ROI**), calculated using this formula:

$$\text{Return on investment (\%)} = \frac{\text{Return on investment (£)}}{\text{Cost of investment (£)}} \times 100$$

Return on investment (£) = Financial gain from investment − costs of investment

2) Return on investment measures how **efficient** an investment is — it compares the return from a project to the amount of money that's been invested in it. The **higher** the ROI, the **better**. Companies might set a target value for the ROI of an investment or use it to compare the profitability of two potential investments.

Financial Objectives

Businesses set Objectives for Long-Term Investments and Funding

1) **Capital** is simply wealth in the form of money or other assets owned by a business.

2) **Capital expenditure** (or investment) is the money spent to buy fixed assets.
   These are things that are used over and over again to produce goods or services, like **factories** or **vehicles**.

3) Businesses may set an **investment objective** to help achieve a set amount of capital
   expenditure during a year. E.g. 'Capital expenditure of £150 000 to fund purchase of new
   equipment'. Alternatively a business may wish to reduce capital expenditure.

4) **Capital structure** refers to the way a business raises capital to purchase **assets**.
   A business's capital structure is a combination of its **debt capital** (borrowed funds) and its **equity capital**.
   Equity capital is the capital raised by **selling shares**, and is sometimes known as share capital.

5) A common **capital structure objective** is to set a **debt to equity ratio**, e.g. 1.5:1 after 4 years.
   Sometimes businesses set targets to reduce the proportion of **debt** in their **long-term funding**.

Internal and External factors influence Financial Objectives

There are many factors that influence a company's **ability** to **achieve** its objectives,
and managers need to take these factors into account when they set financial objectives.

Internal factors influencing financial objectives

1) **The overall objectives of the business** — Financial objectives need to be consistent with the
   corporate objectives of the business. E.g. a company with a strong **environmental** standpoint
   might be more interested in minimising its carbon footprint than in maximising its profits.

2) **The status of the business** — New businesses might set **ambitious** targets for revenue because
   they're trying to grow quickly and establish themselves in the marketplace. **Established** companies
   might be satisfied with **smaller** increases in revenue if they're not actively trying to grow.

3) **Other areas of the business** — Financial objectives might be limited by what's happening in other
   departments of the business. E.g. if a business has a **high turnover of sales staff**, an objective to increase
   revenue might be **unrealistic** because experienced staff are needed to encourage customers to spend more.

External factors influencing financial objectives

1) **The availability of finance** — **Cash flow** targets might depend on how easy it is for the business to get **credit**.

2) **Competitors** — If **new competitors** enter the market, or **demand** for competitors' products **increases** (due to a
   special offer or price reduction, etc), a business might set an objective to **cut costs** to be more competitive.

3) **The economy** — In a period of economic **boom**, businesses can set **ambitious** profit targets.
   In a **downturn**, they have to set more **restrained** targets, and they might also set targets to **minimise costs**.

4) **Shareholders** — Shareholders usually want the best possible **return** on their investment —
   this might put pressure on businesses to set objectives to increase **profits** or **dividends**.

5) **Environmental/Ethical influences** — E.g. sourcing fair trade supplies may affect costs objectives.

Practice Questions

Q1 Give an example of a revenue, a profit and a costs objective.

Q2 Why would a business set a cash flow objective?

Q3 Give two external factors that influence a company's financial objectives.

Exam Question

Q1 Greenwood Desks is a new business aiming to create bespoke desks 'to-order' for both businesses
   and individuals. Greenwood Desks promise to use only sustainable resources in the production process,
   and also offer customers a credit period of 6 months. To what extent are cash flow objectives
   the most important objectives for Greenwood Desks? Justify your answer. [12 marks]

We're choosing another location for the wedding — we're re-venueing...

Make sure everything here is clear before moving on — this stuff is pretty important for the rest of the section.
Learn all of the different types of objectives and why they're important, and walk yourself through the internal and
external factors that influence financial objectives — you never know where they'll pop up in the exams. Eesh.

Measuring and Increasing Profit

Revenue and profit are different animals — revenue is the money received from sales, whereas profit is found by deducting costs from the revenue. There are different types of profit though, so cast your eyes over this spread.

Businesses want to Maximise their Profits

1) Most businesses exist to make a **profit** — if a business makes large profits then it is **successful**. Even successful businesses want to **increase profits** and become **more successful**.

2) Businesses **measure** their profits on a regular basis. They **compare** their profits from the current period (usually a year) to the profits from previous periods to measure their **progress**.

3) If profits go **down**, this is **bad news**, even if the business is still making large profits. For example, if a business makes a profit of £100 million in a year, this might sound like good news, but if the previous year's profit was £125 million then it's a **bad sign**.

4) This is why businesses work out the **percentage increase** or **decrease** in their profits from year to year — it makes it easy to see how well they're performing in comparison with other years.

5) If profits are decreasing, the business needs to investigate **why** this is happening and **take action** to fix it.

The formula for measuring the **percentage change in profit** is:

$$\text{Percentage Change in Profit} = \frac{\text{Current Year's Profit} - \text{Previous Year's Profit}}{\text{Previous Year's Profit}} \times 100$$

Businesses use different Methods to Increase Profits

1) Businesses can **improve** their **profits** by increasing their **prices** (if the demand for their products is price inelastic — see p.36-37) or **reducing** their prices to increase **demand** (if demand is price elastic). The **downside** is that increased prices could mean **reduced sales**, and reduced prices may not increase sales.

2) They could also try to **reduce** their **costs of production**. However, reducing production costs may lead to a **lower quality product**, which could damage the number of sales.

3) Businesses may use **advertising** to increase **demand** for a product, which could increase sales and profit. Unfortunately, advertising can be expensive and there is no guarantee that profits will increase.

4) **Improving** the **quality** of a product can reduce costs from returns or from items that are **not** of an acceptable quality for **sale**. This should lead to an increase in profits, as long as the costs of improving the quality don't outweigh the savings.

There are Different Ways of Reporting Profit

The general profit formula given on p.6 is Profit = Total Revenue − Total Costs.

Businesses are interested in **different measures** of profit:

1) **Gross profit** is the amount left over when the **cost of sales** is **subtracted** from **sales revenue**. Cost of sales includes the costs **directly related** to making the product, e.g. the cost of materials.

$$\text{Gross Profit} = \text{Sales Revenue} - \text{Cost of Sales}$$

2) **Operating profit** takes into account all revenues and costs from **regular trading**, but not any revenues or costs from **one-off** events such as the sale or purchase of another business. Operating profit considers both the cost of sales and **operating expenses**, such as administrative expenses. If a company's **gross profit** is **increasing** but its **operating profit** is **decreasing**, it usually means the company is **not controlling** its **costs**.

$$\text{Operating profit} = \text{Sales Revenue} - \text{Cost of Sales} - \text{Operating Expenses}$$

3) **Profit for the year** also takes into consideration profit or loss from **one-off events** and **financial costs**, e.g. interest payments and tax. It's the measure of profit that dividend payments are based on.

$$\text{Profit for the Year} = \text{Operating Profit} + \text{Other Profit} - \text{Net Finance Costs} - \text{Tax}$$

Example

Hannah's Hammers is a small company selling hammers with a floral design. The cost of producing each hammer is **£2**, and they are sold for **£5** each. Hannah also has operating expenses of **£9000** a year.

If Hannah sells **10 000** hammers in a year, her **sales revenue** is 10 000 × £5 = **£50 000**.

Hannah's **gross profit** is £50 000 − (£2 × 10 000) = **£30 000**.

Her **operating profit** is £50 000 − £20 000 − £9000 = **£21 000**.

Measuring and Increasing Profit

Profit Margins show how Profitable a business or product is

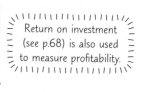

Return on investment (see p.68) is also used to measure profitability.

1) As well as measuring profits, businesses are interested in measuring **profitability** — the amount of profit **relative** to **revenue** or **investment**.

2) Profit margins measure the relationship between the **profit made** and the **sales revenue**. They tell you what **percentage** of the selling price of a product is actually **profit**.

3) Profit margins can be used to make **comparisons** over a period of time, or compare the profitability of different companies.

Gross Profit Margin

1) The **gross profit margin** measures gross profit as a percentage of sales revenue:

$$\text{Gross Profit Margin (\%)} = \frac{\text{Gross Profit}}{\text{Sales Revenue}} \times 100$$

2) What counts as a good gross profit margin depends on the **type of business**, but the **higher** the percentage the better. A business with a high sales volume (e.g. a bakery) can afford to have a low gross profit margin.

3) The margin can be **improved** by **increasing prices** or **reducing** the direct **cost of sales**.

Operating Profit Margin

1) The **operating profit margin** takes into account all the costs of regular trading. Again, it's a percentage:

$$\text{Operating Profit Margin (\%)} = \frac{\text{Operating Profit}}{\text{Sales Revenue}} \times 100$$

2) It's best to have a **high** operating profit margin, although it does depend on the type of business. Operating profits can be **improved** by **increasing prices** or **reducing the cost** of sales or operating expenses.

3) It's useful to **compare** operating profit margin with gross profit margin over a **period of time**. A business with a **decreasing operating profit margin** compared to gross profit margin is struggling with operating expenses.

Profit for the Year Margin

1) The **profit for the year margin** measures the profit for the year as a percentage of sales revenue:

$$\text{Profit for the Year Margin (\%)} = \frac{\text{Profit for the Year}}{\text{Sales Revenue}} \times 100$$

2) A high profit for the year margin is attractive to **shareholders**, because it can indicate that they may receive high dividends. Similarly this can attract potential shareholders.

Practice Questions

Q1 If a business makes a profit of £50 000 in 2018 and £52 000 in 2019, what is the percentage change in profit?

Q2 Calculate the profit for the year for Hannah's Hammers (see previous page), given that the business paid tax of £6000, made £3000 profit from sales of assets and had net finance costs of £2000.

Q3 Give two ways in which the gross profit margin can be improved.

Answers on p.107.

Exam Questions

Q1 Dogs4eva had a gross profit margin of 18% in 2013 and 11% in 2014. Analyse how the company's revenue and costs may have changed from 2013 to 2014. [6 marks]

Q2 A business has sales revenue of £2 million. Its gross profit is £750 000, and its operating expenses are £250 000.
a) Calculate the operating profit margin. [4 marks]
b) Analyse what the business could do to improve the operating profit margin. [9 marks]

I'm just about 100% fed up with all these percentage calculations...

OK, I admit this hasn't been the world's most interesting page but this is all really important stuff, so make sure you get your head around it before moving on. You need to be able to calculate the profits and their margins, so learn the formulas. You also need to understand what they mean for a business and how firms can improve their profitability.

Cash Flow Forecasting

Remember cash flow (p.68)? Well, cash flow forecasts are dead important for businesses. They're used to predict when money will come in and out of the business over a period of time, and can help prevent nasty monetary surprises.

The **Cash Flow Cycle** is the **Gap** between **Money Going Out** and **Coming In**

1) Cash **inflows** are sums of money **received** by a business, e.g. from product sales or loans.
Cash **outflows** are sums of money **paid out** by a business, e.g. to buy raw materials, or pay wages.

2) Businesses need to **pay out money** for the costs of producing an order, or for assets like machinery, **before** they **get paid** for that order. This **delay** between money going out and money coming in is called the **cash flow cycle**.

3) It's important to make sure there's always **enough money** available to make payments. Not paying suppliers and employees can be something of a **disaster**. For **new businesses** the cash flow cycle can be a **big problem** because they need money for **start-up costs** before they've made any sales at all. The money available to a business for its day-to-day running costs is called **working capital**.

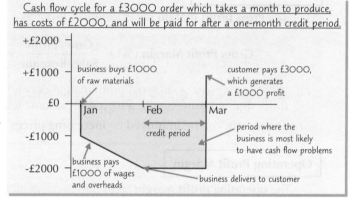

Cash flow cycle for a £3000 order which takes a month to produce, has costs of £2000, and will be paid for after a one-month credit period.

4) The **length** of the **cash flow cycle** depends on:

• **The type of product** — this determines the **length of time** it takes to produce and **how long** it's held in stock. E.g. a butcher wouldn't hold stock for long, so there would only be a short delay between paying suppliers and selling to customers.

• **Credit payments** — Buying **on credit** means that the goods are received, but the buyer has an agreed period of time (credit period) before payment is due. E.g. a sofa company may allow customers three months from the purchase date to pay for their sofa. Businesses also buy **on credit** from their **suppliers**.

5) People who are **owed** money by the business are known as **creditors**. Money that the business owes is known as **payable**. People who **owe** the business money are called **debtors**. Money that is owed to the business is known as **receivable**.

6) The **ideal cash flow situation** is where there's a short period of time from the start of production to the sale of goods, and where the business is given a longer credit period by its creditors (e.g. suppliers) than it gives its debtors (e.g. customers).

Businesses have **Various Canny Tricks** to **Improve** Cash Flow

Businesses have various methods to **improve cash flow**, but they can have **drawbacks**.

1) **Overdrafts** can be arranged with banks to allow a business to borrow money according to its needs, up to a preset amount. These can be useful in times of need, but in the long term overdrafts can be very **expensive**, as the business will need to pay **interest** on the borrowed money.

2) Businesses can try to hold less **stock**, so less **cash** is tied up in stock. But this could cause problems if there is a sudden increase in demand for a product, as they may run out.

3) Businesses try to **reduce the time** between **paying** suppliers and **getting money** from customers. They try to get their **suppliers** to give them a **longer** credit period — and give their **customers** a **shorter** credit period. However it's important to **balance** the need to manage cash flow with the need to keep suppliers and customers **happy** — you don't want customers to go elsewhere.

4) **Credit controllers** keep **debtors** in control. They set credit limits and remind debtors to pay up.

5) **Debt factoring** gives instant cash to businesses whose customers haven't paid their invoices. Banks and other financial institutions act as **debt factoring agents**. The agent pays the business about **80%** of the value of the invoice as an **instant cash advance**. The agent gets the customer to pay up, and then **keeps** about **5%** of the value of the invoice — debt factoring costs money and the agent needs to make a living.

6) **Sale and leaseback** is when businesses **sell** equipment to **raise capital**, and then **lease** (rent) the equipment back. That way, they get a big **lump sum** from the sale, and pay a **little** bit of money each month for the lease of the equipment. Of course, they don't get to own the equipment again unless they get enough cash to buy it back — and they have to pay the lease in the meantime.

Cash Flow Forecasting

Businesses make Cash Flow Forecasts to help them make Decisions

1) **Cash flow forecasts** (also called cash budgets) show the amount of money that managers **expect** to **flow into** the business and **flow out** of the business over a period of time in the **future**.

2) Managers can use cash flow forecasts to **make sure** they always have **enough** cash around to pay **suppliers** and **employees**. They can **predict** when they'll be **short of cash**, and arrange a **loan** or **overdraft** in time.

3) Businesses show cash flow forecasts to **banks** and venture capitalists when trying to get **loans** and other finance. Cash flow forecasts prove that a business has an idea of where it's going to be in the future.

4) They can be used to check that a firm isn't holding **too much cash**, i.e. cash that could be invested in the business instead.

5) **Established** firms base forecasts on **past experience**. **New** firms have no past data, so their forecast should consider the business's **capacity**, experiences of **similar firms** and customer trends shown by **market research**.

Example: A new firm starts up with a loan of £18 000 and £5000 of capital. It expects to sell £5000 of goods in January, £35 000 in February, £35 000 in March and £40 000 in April. All customers will get a **one month credit period**. Wages and rent will cost £15 000 in total each month, and other costs are expected to be £5000 in January, £8000 in February, £2000 in March and £2000 in April.

This shows cash coming in from sales and from the initial start-up loan. → **Cash in**

This shows cash going out to pay for the firm's costs. → **Cash out**

Net cash flow = cash inflows − cash outflows → **Net monthly cash flow**

Item	Jan	Feb	Mar	Apr
Sales revenue		£5000	£35000	£35000
Other cash in	£18000			
Total cash inflows	**£18000**	**£5000**	**£35000**	**£35000**
Wages and rent	£15000	£15000	£15000	£15000
Other costs	£5000	£8000	£2000	£2000
Total cash outflows	**£20000**	**£23000**	**£17000**	**£17000**
Net cash flow	(£2000)	(£18000)	£18000	£18000
Opening balance	£5000	£3000	(£15000)	£3000
Closing balance	£3000	(£15000)	£3000	£21000

There's a one month credit period, so each month's sales revenue isn't received until the following month.

Figures in brackets are negative.

According to this, the business will have £21 000 in the bank by the end of April. But it'll still owe £18 000 from the start-up loan...

The opening balance is money in the bank at the start — for January it's £5000.

Closing balance = opening balance + net cash flow

The closing balance for last month is this month's opening balance.

Cash Flow Forecasting isn't always accurate

1) Cash flow forecasts can be based on **false assumptions** about what's going to happen.

2) Circumstances can **change suddenly** after the forecast's been made. **Costs** can **go up**. Machinery can **break down** and need mending. **Competitors** can put their prices up or down, which **affects sales**.

3) Good cash flow forecasting needs lots of **experience** and lots of **research** into the market.

4) A **false forecast** can have **disastrous** results. A business that runs out of cash could end up **insolvent**.

Practice Questions

Q1 Give two methods a business may use to improve cash flow.

Q2 Give two reasons why a cash flow forecast is useful to someone setting up their own small business.

Q3 If a company has a total cash in of £8000 and a total cash out of £9500, what is its net cash flow?

Q4 If a company has an opening balance of £20 000 and its net cash flow is (£7000), what is the closing balance?

Q5 How can you work out a company's opening balance in any given month?

Answers on p.107.

Exam Questions

Q1 Analyse the ways in which a car sales company could improve its cash flow. [9 marks]

Q2 To what extent can a business successfully and accurately predict future cash flow? Explain your answer. [12 marks]

Dunno 'bout you, but cash flows through my wallet like water...

Cash flow is important — without it, businesses can end up insolvent and individuals could go bankrupt. Make sure you know how to calculate the figures in the forecast on this page. It can be tricky to start with, so go over it a few times if you need to. Don't forget to learn the ways that businesses can improve cash flow. It'll be worth it in the exams.

Setting Budgets

Businesses make financial plans. They set targets for how much money they're going to make, and how much they're going to spend. Then they check to see how they've done. It sounds simple enough...

A **Budget** is a **Financial Plan** for the future

A **budget** forecasts **future earnings** and **future spending**, usually over a 12 month period. Businesses use different budgets to estimate different things. There are three types of budget:

Marketing data is used in financial planning.

1) **Income budgets** forecast the amount of money that will come into the company as revenue. In order to do this, the company needs to predict **how much** it will sell, and at what **price**. Managers estimate this using their **sales figures** from previous years, as well as **market research.**

2) **Expenditure budgets** predict what the business's **total costs** will be for the year, taking into account both fixed and variable costs. Variable costs increase with output, so managers must predict output based on sales estimates.

3) The **profit budget** uses the **income budget** minus the **expenditure budget** to calculate what the expected **profit** (or **loss**) will be for that year.

Budgets affect **All Areas** of the business

1) The expenditure budget forecasts **total** expenditure. This is broken down into **department** expenditure budgets — each department is allotted a certain amount of money to spend.

2) **Budget holders** are people **responsible** for spending or generating the money for each budget. For example, the budget holder of the expenditure budget for marketing could be the head of the marketing department.

3) Department expenditure budgets are broken down into budgets for **specific activities** within the department. These help local managers control and coordinate their work.

Item of Expenditure	Expenditure (£)
Wages	150 000
Marketing	50 000
Raw Materials	100 000
Research and Development	25 000
Total Expenditure	**325 000**

The **Budget Setting** process involves **Research** and **Negotiation**

1) To set the **income budget**, businesses **research** and **predict** how sales are going to go up and down through the year, so that they can make a good prediction of **sales revenue**.

2) To set the **expenditure budget** for **production**, businesses research how labour costs, raw materials costs, taxes and inflation are going to go up over the year. They can then figure out the **costs** of producing the volume of product that they think they're going to sell.

3) **Budgets** are **influenced** by a company's **objectives** — e.g. if they aim to increase sales, this will affect their predicted sales revenue and cost of sales, and they might allocate more of the expenditure budget to marketing.

4) Annual budgets are usually agreed by **negotiation** — when budget holders have a say in setting their budgets, they're **motivated** to achieve them.

5) Budgets should **stretch** the abilities of the business, but they must be **achievable**. **Unrealistically** high income budgets or low expenditure budgets will **demotivate** staff. No one likes being asked to do the **impossible**.

6) Once they've agreed the budget, budget holders **keep checking** performance against the budget. This is called **variance analysis**. There's more about variance and variance analysis on p.76-77.

Budgets have **Advantages** and **Disadvantages**

Benefits of budgeting

- Budgets help to **achieve targets**, like keeping costs low or revenue high.
- Budgets help **control** income and expenditure. They show where the money goes.
- Budgeting helps managers to **review** their activities and make decisions.
- Budgeting helps focus on the **priorities**.
- Budgets let heads of department **delegate** authority to budget holders. Getting authority is **motivating**.
- Budgets allow departments to **coordinate** spending.
- Budgets help persuade **investors** that the business will be successful.

Drawbacks of budgeting

- Budgeting can cause **resentment** and rivalry if departments have to compete for money.
- Budgets can be **restrictive**. Fixed budgets stop firms responding to changing market conditions.
- Budgeting is **time-consuming**. Managers can get too preoccupied with setting and reviewing budgets, and forget to focus on the real issues of **winning business** and **understanding** the **customer**.
- **Inflation** is difficult to predict — some prices can change by levels much **greater** than average.
- Start-up businesses may struggle to gather data from other firms, so the budget may be **inaccurate**.

Setting Budgets

Budgets can be *Updated Every Year* or developed from *Scratch*

1) **Start-up businesses** have to develop their budgets **from scratch** (known as **zero-based budgeting**). This is difficult to do because they don't have much information to base their decisions on — they can't take into account the previous year's sales or expenditure. This means that their budgets are likely to be **inaccurate**.

2) After the first year, a business must decide whether to follow the **historical budgeting** method, or to continue using the **zero-based budgeting** method.

Historical budgets are updated each year

1) This year's budget is based on a percentage increase or decrease from last year's budget. For example, a business expecting 10% revenue growth might add 10% to the advertising, wages and raw materials purchasing budgets.

2) Historical budgeting is **quick** and **simple**, but it assumes that business conditions stay **unchanged** each year. This isn't always the case — for instance, a product at the introduction stage of its **life cycle** (see p.44) needs more money spent on advertising than one in the growth or maturity stages.

Zero-based budgeting means starting from scratch each year

1) Budget holders **start** with a budget of **£0**, and have to **get approval** to spend money on activities.

2) They have to **plan** all the year's activities, ask for money to spend on them, and be prepared to **justify** their requests to the finance director. Budget holders need good **negotiating** skills for this.

3) Zero-based budgeting takes much **longer** to complete than historical budgets.

4) If zero-based budgeting is done properly it's **more accurate** than historical budgeting.

Budgets affect how *Flexible* a business can be

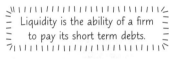
Liquidity is the ability of a firm to pay its short term debts.

1) **Fixed budgets** provide **discipline** and **certainty**. This is especially important for a business with **liquidity** problems — fixed budgets help control **cash flow**.

2) **Fixed budgeting** means budget holders have to stick to their budget plans throughout the year — even if market conditions change. This can **prevent** a firm reacting to **new opportunities** or **threats** that they didn't know about when they set the budget.

3) **Flexible budgeting** allows budgets to be altered in response to significant changes in the market or economy.

4) **Zero-based budgeting** gives a business more **flexibility** than **historical budgeting**.

Mary had no problems with flexibility

Practice Questions

Q1 Name the three main types of budget that a business will set, stating what each tells you.
Q2 If a business has an income budget of £125 000 and a profit budget of £30 000, what is its expenditure budget?
Q3 State three benefits and three drawbacks of using budgets.
Q4 What is historical budgeting?
Q5 Explain the difference between fixed and flexible budgets.

Answer on p.107.

Exam Questions

Q1 To what extent might fixed budgets help a manufacturer in the fast-changing computer software sector? [16 marks]

Q2 a) Explain the benefits that setting a budget will have for a new business. [6 marks]
   b) Analyse the problems that a new business might have in setting budgets for the first time. [9 marks]

I set myself a word budget today and I'm just about to run out...

Budgets are multi-purpose — they help businesses forecast their future spending and they can help to motivate people. Make sure you know how they're constructed and how to explain their benefits and drawbacks.

Analysing Budgets

Budgets are often reviewed using variance analysis. Variance is the difference between actual and budgeted spend.
Understanding variances helps managers make decisions and fix problems, and it'll help you sail through your exams.

Variance is the Difference between Actual figures and Budgeted figures

1) A variance means the business is performing either **worse** or **better** than expected.

2) A **favourable variance** leads to **increased profit**. If revenue's more than the budget says it's going to be, that's a favourable variance. If costs are below the cost predictions in the budget, that's a favourable variance.

3) An **adverse variance** is a difference that **reduces profits**. **Selling fewer items** than the income budget predicts or **spending more** on an advert than the expenditure budget for marketing allows is an adverse variance.

4) If £10 000 is spent on raw materials in a month when the budget was only £6000, the variance is £6000 − £10 000 = −£4000, so there is a £4000 **adverse variance**.

5) Variances **add up**. For example, if actual sales exceed budgeted sales by £3000 and expenditure on raw materials is £2000 below budget, the variance is £3000 + £2000 = £5000, so there's a combined **favourable variance** of £5000. This is called **cumulative variance**.

6) Variances can be calculated for each budget each month, for each budget as a running total, and for groups of budgets as a monthly or running total variance:

> (A) means an adverse variance.
> (F) means a favourable variance.

	Jan Budget	Jan Actual	Jan Variance	Feb Budget	Feb Actual	Feb Variance	Cumulative Variance
Revenue	£100k	£90k	£10k (A)	£110k	£110k	£0	£10k (A)
Wages	£40k	£30k	£10k (F)	£40k	£41k	£1k (A)	£9k (F)
Rent	£10k	£10k	£0	£10k	£11k	£1k (A)	£1k (A)
Other costs	£5k	£6k	£1k (A)	£5k	£6k	£1k (A)	£2k (A)
Total costs	£55k	£46k	£9k (F)	£55k	£58k	£3k (A)	£6k (F)

Variances can be Bad — even if they say you're doing Better than Expected

1) When variances occur, it means that what has happened is **not** what the business was expecting. Businesses need to **know** about variances so that they can find out **why** they have occurred.

2) It's extremely important to spot **adverse** variances as **soon** as possible. It's important to find out which budget holder is responsible — and to take action to fix the problem.

3) It's **also** important to **investigate favourable variances**. Favourable variances may mean that the budget targets weren't **stretching** enough — so the business needs to set more **difficult targets**. The business also needs to understand **why** the performance is better than expected — if one department is **doing something right**, the business can **spread** this throughout the organisation.

Variances are caused by several factors, both Internal and External

External Factors Cause Variance

1) **Competitor behaviour** and changing **fashions** may increase or reduce **demand** for products.
2) Changes in the **economy** can change how much workers' wages cost the business.
3) The cost of **raw materials** can go up — e.g. if a harvest fails.

Internal Factors Cause Variance

1) Improving **efficiency** (e.g. by introducing automated production equipment) causes **favourable** variances.
2) A business might **overestimate** the amount of money it can save by streamlining its production methods.
3) A business might **underestimate** the **cost** of making a change to its organisation.
4) Changing the **selling price** changes sales revenue — this creates variance if it happens after the budget's set.
5) Internal causes of variance are a **big concern**. They suggest that internal **communication** needs improving.

Analysing Budgets

Variance Analysis means Identifying and Explaining variances

1) Variance analysis means **spotting** variances and figuring out **why** they've happened, so that action can be taken to fix them.

2) **Small** variances aren't a big problem. They can actually help to **motivate** employees. Staff try to **catch up** and sort out small **adverse** variances themselves. Small **favourable** variances can motivate staff to **keep on** doing whatever they were doing to create a favourable variance.

3) **Large** variances can **demotivate**. Staff don't work hard if there are large favourable variances — they **don't see the need**. Staff can get demotivated by a large **adverse** variance — they may feel that the task is **impossible**, or that they've **already failed**.

Businesses have to React to variances

When variances occur, businesses need to act on them. They can either change what the **business** is doing to make it fit the budget, or change the **budget** to make it fit what the **business** is doing. There are three factors that they need to take into account to make this decision:

1) Businesses need to **beware** of chopping and changing the budget **too much**.

2) Changing the budget **removes certainty** — which removes one of the big benefits of budgets.

3) Altering budgets can also make them **less motivating** — when staff start to expect that management will change targets instead of doing something to change performance, they don't see the point in trying any more.

Decisions based on Adverse Variances

1) They can change the **marketing mix**.
Cutting prices will increase sales — but only if the demand is price elastic (see p.36).
Updating the product might make it more attractive to customers. Businesses can also look for a **new market** for the product, or change the **promotional strategy** — e.g. by advertising the product more or doing point of sales promotion.

2) **Streamlining production** makes the business more **efficient**, so this reduces costs.

3) They can try to motivate **employees** to **work harder**.

4) Businesses can try to cut costs by asking their **suppliers** for a **better deal**.

5) Businesses may need to do additional **market research** to improve their forecasts in the future.

Decisions based on Favourable Variances

1) If the favourable variance is caused by a **pessimistic** budget, they can set more **ambitious targets** next time.

2) If the variance is because of **increased productivity** in one part of the business, they can try to get everyone else doing whatever was **responsible** for the improvement, and set higher targets in the next budget.

3) A favourable variance could indicate more **sales** than predicted, so a business may need to increase the **production** of a product or take on additional staff to meet demand.

Practice Questions

Q1 Define variance.

Q2 If a business sets an expenditure budget of £15 000 for marketing and the actual expenditure for marketing is £18 000, how much is the variance and what type of variance is it?

Q3 Why are variances a concern for businesses?

Q4 How do businesses deal with variances?

Answers on p.107.

Exam Question

Q1 a) Using the figures in the table on p.76, calculate monthly and cumulative variances for March. Assume all budgets remain the same as February, and that actual sales are £120k, wages are £39k, rent is £11k and other costs are £5k. [10 marks]

b) Explain what your answer to a) suggests about the budget planning process for this company. [6 marks]

Variance is one of those words that looks odd if you stare at it enough...

Variance variance variance... ahem... anyway. As well as knowing what businesses do when they set a budget, you need to know what they do when the real-life results don't quite match up to what the budget says. They don't panic and run about shouting "beeble beeble" in the car park. They just sort it out so it doesn't happen next time.

Break-Even Analysis

Break-even analysis is a great way of working out how much you need to sell to make a profit.

Breaking Even means Covering your Costs

1) The **break-even output** is the level of sales a business needs to **cover its costs**.
   At the break-even point, costs = revenue.

2) When sales are **below** the break-even output, costs are more than revenue — the business makes a **loss**.
   When sales are **above** the break-even output, revenue exceeds costs — the business makes a **profit**.

3) **New businesses** should always do a **break-even analysis** to **find** the break-even output.
   It tells them how much they will need to sell to break even. Banks and venture capitalists
   thinking of **loaning** money to the business will need to **see** a break-even analysis as part of
   the **business plan**. This helps them to decide whether to lend money to the business.

4) **Established businesses** preparing to launch **new products** use break-even analysis to work out how much
   profit they are likely to make, and also to predict the impact of the new activity on **cash flow** (see p.72-73).

Contribution is used to work out the Break-Even Output

1) **Contribution** is the difference between the **selling price** of a product and the **variable costs** it takes to produce it.

   | Contribution per unit = selling price per unit – variable costs per unit |

   See p.6 for more on fixed and variable costs.

2) The **total contribution** is worked out using one of the two formulas below:

   | Total contribution = total revenue – total variable costs OR contribution per unit × number of units sold |

3) Contribution is used to **pay fixed costs**. The amount left over is profit.

4) **The break-even output** is where **contribution = fixed costs**.
   You calculate it using this formula:

   $$\text{Break-even output} = \frac{\text{fixed costs}}{\text{contribution per unit}}$$

Example: Harry sets up a business to print T-shirts. The **fixed costs** of premises and the T-shirt printers are **£3000**.
The **variable costs** per T-shirt (the T-shirt, ink, wages) are **£5**. Each printed T-shirt sells for **£25**.

Contribution per unit = £25 – £5 = **£20**

Break-even output = £3000 ÷ £20 = **150**   So, Harry has to sell **150** T-shirts to **break even**.

Draw a Break-Even Chart to show the Break-Even Output

1) Break-even charts show **costs** and **revenue** plotted against
   output. Businesses use break-even charts to see how costs
   and revenue **vary** with different levels of output.

2) **Output** goes on the **horizontal axis**. The scale needs to
   let you plot output from 0 to the maximum possible.

3) **Costs and revenue** both go on the vertical axis. Use a scale
   that lets you plot from 0 to the maximum revenue.

4) Plot **fixed** costs. (On the diagram on the right, fixed costs are
   the blue horizontal line.) **Add** variable costs to fixed costs to
   get the **total costs**, and plot them on the graph.
   (The total costs are shown by the purple line, starting at the same point as the fixed costs line.)

5) Next, plot **revenue** (selling price × number of units) on the graph. (It's the green line on the diagram.)

6) The **break-even output** is where the **revenue** line crosses the **total costs** line. On the diagram it's 150 units.

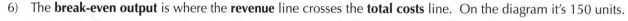

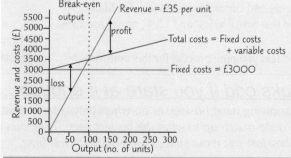

Changing either the variable costs or the price of the
products will affect the break-even output.

This graph shows that if Harry **increased the price**
of the T-shirts to £35 each, his break-even output
would be **lowered** to 100 units.

When **prices increase**, the **revenue line** gets **steeper**,
so the break-even output is **lowered** — if you **charge**
more, you don't need to sell as **many** to break even.

Break-Even Analysis

Margin of safety = actual output – break-even output

1) The diagram on the right shows the margin of safety for Harry's T-shirt business when his output is 250 T-shirts. If Harry sells **250** T-shirts, the **margin of safety** is 250 – 150 = **100**. He could sell up to 100 fewer T-shirts before he started losing money.

2) If his output changed to **300** T-shirts, the margin of safety would go up to 300 – 150 = **150**.

3) Knowing the break-even output and margin of safety allows businesses to make **important decisions** — if Harry's calculations show that his T-shirt business has a low margin of safety, he can take action to increase it by either **lowering his costs** or **increasing his revenue**.

4) This would **lower** his break-even output, so he'd have a **greater** margin of safety. A big margin of safety is useful for a business because it means less risk.

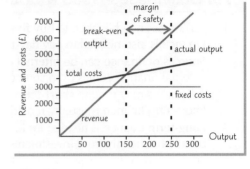

Break-Even Analysis has **Advantages** and **Disadvantages**

Advantages of break-even analysis	Disadvantages of break-even analysis
It's **easy** to do. If you can plot figures on a graph accurately, you can do break-even analysis.	Break-even analysis assumes that **variable costs** always rise steadily. This isn't always the case — a business can get **discounts** for buying in bulk so costs don't go up in **direct proportion** to output.
It's **quick** — managers can see the **break-even output** and **margin of safety** immediately so they can take **quick action** to cut costs or increase sales if they need to **increase** their margin of safety.	Break-even analysis is simple for a **single product** — but most businesses sell lots of different products, so looking at the business as a whole can get a lot more complicated.
Break-even charts let businesses **forecast** how variations in sales will affect **costs**, **revenue** and **profits** and, most importantly, how variations in **price** and **costs** will affect how **much** they **need** to **sell**.	If the **data** is wrong, then the **results** will be wrong.
Businesses can use break-even analysis to help **persuade** the bank to give them a **loan**.	Break-even analysis assumes the business sells **all the products**, without any wastage. But, for example, a restaurant business will end up throwing away food if fewer customers turn up than they're expecting.
Break-even analysis influences decisions on whether **new products** are launched or not — if the business would need to sell an unrealistic volume of products to break even, they would probably decide **not** to launch the product.	Break-even analysis only tells you how many units you **need** to sell to break even. It doesn't tell you how many you're **actually going to sell**.

Practice Questions

Q1 Write down the formulas for contribution per unit, total contribution and break-even output.

Q2 Write down two advantages and two disadvantages of break-even analysis.

Exam Questions

Q1 Bob is deciding whether to set up a business selling fishing equipment. Evaluate the value of break-even analysis in helping Bob decide whether or not to go ahead with the business. [12 marks]

Q2 Muneer Khan has a small restaurant. The average price per customer per meal is £13. The variable costs of materials and labour per meal are £5. The fixed costs of the restaurant are £1000 per month. Calculate the break-even number of customers per month. Answer on p.107. [4 marks]

Ah, give us a break...

You might be asked to calculate the break-even output or draw it on a graph, so make sure you can do both. Make sure you can give examples of how break-even analysis is used by businesses to make decisions and plans, and learn some advantages and disadvantages of break-even analysis. Then give yourself a pat on the back. Yippee...

Choosing Sources of Finance

There are loads of different sources of finance for businesses, each with advantages and disadvantages.
A business must choose carefully depending on what they need the money for and what's available to them.

All Businesses Need a Source of Finance

1) Businesses need finance to buy **fixed assets**, like factories, offices and machinery.
   Finance is also needed to pay **day-to-day costs**, like wages and bills, so that the business can survive.
2) Sources of finance can be **internal** or **external**. Internal finance is money from **within** the business, e.g. profit.
   External finance comes from sources **outside** the business, like bank loans or shareholder investments.
3) A business may require **short-term** finance to pay its suppliers or cover **temporary** shortages of cash.
   Short-term finance is usually repaid within **1 year**.
4) **Long-term** finance is needed for long-term investment. It can take a while for a business to
   benefit financially from investments like new machinery, so repayments of long-term finance
   are due over a **longer period**, usually 3 years or more.
5) When **choosing** a source of finance, a business must consider various things, including:

- **The legal structure of the business** — limited companies can sell shares, but this isn't an option for sole traders.
- **The amount of money required** — the larger the amount, the less likely it is that internal finance can be raised.
- **The level of risk involved** — a risky business is less likely to find a loan, although venture capital is an option.
- **If short-term or long-term finance is needed** — it depends on how long it will take the business to repay it.

Internal Finance comes from Within the business

Internal finance can be raised by putting **profits** back into the business, or **selling assets**.

Retained profit

1) **Profit** can be retained and built up over the years for **later investment**. This can work in the **short and long term**.
2) The main **benefit** of using profit for investment is that the business doesn't have to pay **interest** on the money.
   Not all businesses can use this method though — they might not be making enough **profit**.
3) **Shareholders** may object to this method as they may wish to receive the profits as **dividends**.
   Also, retaining profits may cause the business to **miss out** on investment opportunities.

Rationalisation

1) **Rationalisation** is when managers **reorganise** the business to make it more efficient. They can do this by **selling**
   some of their **assets** (e.g. factories, machinery, etc) to generate capital, then leasing them back when required.
2) Businesses don't need to pay **interest** on finance they raise by selling their assets.
3) The main **drawback** to selling assets is that the business **no longer owns** the asset. And leasing the asset back
   introduces another cost to the business. Also, assets like cars and computers **lose value** over time, so the
   business won't get back as much as it paid for them.

Some External Sources are suitable as Short-Term Finance

Overdrafts

1) **Overdrafts** are where a bank lets a business have a **negative** amount of money in its bank account.
2) Overdrafts are **easy to arrange** and **flexible** — businesses can borrow as **little** or as **much** as they need
   (up to the overdraft limit) and they only pay **interest** on the amount of the overdraft they actually use.
3) The main **disadvantage** of overdrafts is that banks charge **high rates** of **interest** on them. There may
   also be a **fixed charge** for using an overdraft. So they're **unsuitable** for using in the **long term**.

Debt factoring

1) **Debt factoring** is when banks and other financial institutions take **unpaid invoices** off the hands of
   the business, and give them an instant **cash** payment (of less than 100% of the value of the invoice).
2) The **advantage** of this for businesses is that they can **instantly** get money they are owed.
3) The **disadvantage** of debt factoring is that the debt factoring company **keeps** some of the money owed as a **fee**.

Choosing Sources of Finance

Businesses can take out *Loans* to finance their projects in the *Long-Term*

1) Bank loans are an **external** source of finance. Businesses can borrow a fixed amount of **money** and pay it back over a fixed period of **time** with **interest** — the amount they have to pay back depends on the interest rate and the length of time the loan is for.

2) Banks need **security** for a loan, usually in the form of property.

3) Loans are a good **long-term** source of finance for a **start-up** business and for paying for **assets** like machinery and computers. They are **not** a good way to cover the **day-to-day** running costs of the business.

Advantages of bank loans	Disadvantages of bank loans
1) You're **guaranteed** the money for the duration of the loan (the bank can't suddenly demand it back). 2) You only have to pay back the **loan** and **interest** — the bank won't **own** any of your business and you don't have to give them a share of the **profits**. 3) The interest charges for a loan are usually **lower** than for an overdraft.	1) They can be **difficult** to arrange because a bank will only lend a business money if they think they are going to get it back. If the business doesn't own any property or other assets that can be used for security, they might not be able to get a loan. 2) Keeping up with the **repayments** can be difficult if cash isn't coming into the business quickly enough. The business might **lose** whatever the loan is secured on (e.g. their home) — the bank can sell it to get their money back. 3) The business might have to pay a **charge** if they decide to pay the loan back **early**.

Share Capital is an External Source of Finance for Limited Companies

1) **Private and public limited companies** can be financed in the **long-term** using **ordinary share capital** — money raised by selling **shares** in the business (see p.10).

2) Using share capital to finance a business has its **advantages**. E.g. the money **doesn't** need to be **repaid** (unlike a loan) and new shareholders can bring additional expertise into a business.

3) The **drawback** of selling shares is that the original owner(s) no longer **owns** all of the business — they may have to pay the shareholders a **dividend** (depending on profit) and also give them a **say** in how the business is run.

Venture Capital and Crowdfunding are Other Sources of External Finance

1) **Venture capital** is funding in the form of share or loan capital that is invested in a business that is thought to be high risk. **Venture capitalists** are professional investors who invest in businesses they think have the potential to be successful. They may also provide **business advice**, but applying for funding is a **long** process.

2) **Crowdfunding** is a method of financing a business or project using contributions made by a **large number of people**, usually done via the **internet** through organisations such as Kickstarter and Crowdcube. Contributors can give donations, loans or buy shares, depending on the business.

3) **Rewards** are sometimes offered for donations, such as early access to a product, or the product at a discounted price upon release. These can **reduce profits** if not controlled carefully. The crowdfunding organisations often take a small portion of the finance raised too, meaning not all of it reaches the crowdfunded business.

Practice Questions

Q1 What is internal finance?

Q2 What is the difference between an overdraft and a loan?

Q3 What is meant by the term venture capital?

The Caterham Formula 1 team used crowdfunding in November 2014 to raise money to enter the team in the Abu Dhabi Grand Prix after going into administration.

Exam Questions

Q1 Which of the following sources of finance is an internal source? [1 mark]

    A Retained profit   B Crowdfunding   C Debt Factoring   D Overdrafts

Q2 Discuss the advantages and disadvantages of financing a new business using a bank loan. [9 marks]

"Doctor, I've swallowed my wallet" — a classic example of internal finance...

Sources of finance might not be the most exciting topic in the world, but it's really important for businesses. Nearly all businesses set out to make a profit, and if they can't get enough money to pay for day-to-day survival, they won't last very long at all. Make sure you're clear on all the different ways that businesses can raise internal and external finance.

Human Resource Objectives

These pages are all about managing "human resources" — otherwise known as people.

Human Resource Management is about Managing People

1) The purpose of Human Resource Management (HRM) is to ensure that a business achieves the **maximum benefit** from its employees at the **minimum cost**. The human resources (HR) department needs to make sure that the business has the right **number of employees** with the right **skills**, **qualifications** and **qualities**.

2) Human Resource (HR) objectives are influenced by the objectives of the business **as a whole**. E.g. if the business is going to expand into a new market, the HR department might need to **recruit new staff** to suit the business needs.

3) They also work closely with **other departments**. These departments help HR to anticipate **workforce needs** and react to them — by **recruiting** new staff or **providing training**. HR needs to work with the finance department to determine a **suitable budget** for the department.

4) HR also decides how to treat staff — how to **use their skills**, how to **keep** them working for the company, how to **train** and **reward** them, and eventually how to **terminate** their employment.

Objectives help HR to Manage People Effectively

HR objectives help HR to manage staff successfully. Objectives for the HR department might include:

1 — Matching the Workforce to Business Needs

- HR needs to anticipate the **future size** of the workforce — if the organisation is **expanding** they'll need more workers, if it's **contracting** they won't need as many.
- They decide what **skill-level** the workforce **needs**, and whether staff should be employed **full-** or **part-time**. If the requirements of the business change, HR can decide whether to **train** current staff or **recruit** new workers from **outside** the business.
- They also work with other managers to decide **where** employees are needed if a business has several sites or branches, and **which departments** within a business require specific staff.
- HR also needs to think about **diversity** in all positions of the business, from **floor staff** to **directors**. A workforce that is diverse in **age**, **gender** and **race** will have a wide variety of skills, ideas and experiences.
- HR has a **budget** like all other departments. They have to make sure that staff wages are **appropriate** to the job and employee. They focus on getting the **right balance** between staying within the budget and having the **correct number** of staff, the right amount of **training** and **rewarding** more skilled/senior positions.

2 — Helping Employees Reach their Full Potential

- HR invests in **training** so workers can improve their **productivity**. They also make sure that employees have the right **equipment** to do their job properly.
- HR makes sure there are opportunities for **career progression**. Employees work better and are more **engaged** if they have **something to aim for**, like a **promotion** or taking on extra responsibility at work.
- In certain businesses, HR needs to make sure they focus on the **most talented** employees reaching their **full potential**. This can be achieved through extra **training** and 'fast-tracking' schemes.
- They need to match **workforce skill-levels** to jobs. If a job is too **challenging** for an employee, this can lead to **demotivation** and **low self-esteem**. If the work is too easy, employees become **bored**.
- Effective **management**, good staff **organisation** and a pleasant **working environment** help to improve **morale** — happy employees are more likely to work to their full potential.

3 — Supporting Employee/Employer Relations

- Employee/employer relations are based upon **good communication**. HR **listens** and **reacts** to employee concerns. They can **advise** managers how to deal with problems in their departments.
- Employees who are given **responsibility** and are **involved** in decision-making feel **valued** and **trusted**.
- Improving the **relationship** between employees and management can reduce **absenteeism** and **labour turnover**. If employees feel **engaged**, they're more likely to be **loyal** to the business.
- **Breakdown in relations** can lead to **decreased productivity**, **low morale** and even **strike** action.
- Employee/employer relationships work best when the **values** of the employee **align** with the values of the employer. The employee should always bear in mind the values of the employer when making **decisions**.

Human Resource Objectives

Internal and External Factors influence HR Objectives

Internal factors

1) The **culture** within the business influences **HR objectives**. E.g. some businesses, like fast food restaurants, might not be worried about having a high labour turnover, so they wouldn't want HR to spend time and money trying to reduce it.

2) Other **departments** within the business influence HR. They give HR the information that they need to **predict** workforce needs.

3) The amount of **funding** available within the business.

External factors

1) The general state of the **economy** (boom or recession) will affect HR activities such as **recruitment** and **training**.

2) All UK businesses are subject to **UK** and **EU employment laws**. HR might have to change their objectives to fit in with **new legislation**.

3) Current **ethical** and **environmental** issues can influence HR objectives, e.g. the condemning of **zero-hours contracts**.

4) Improvements in **technology** might mean HR **recruit** people who can use a certain type of software or machine.

HRM Approaches can be Hard or Soft

There are **two schools of thought** in human resource management — **hard HRM** and **soft HRM**.

Hard HRM

1) Employees are seen as a **resource** like any other.

2) Employees are hired on a **short-term basis**.

3) Managers believe that employees are mainly motivated by **money** and think they will do as **little** work as possible.

4) Appraisals are **judgemental**.

5) Training is only done to meet **production** needs.

Soft HRM

1) Employees are the **most important** resource.

2) Employees are managed on a **long-term basis**.

3) Managers motivate employees through **empowerment** and **development** and think that working is **natural** for employees.

4) Appraisals are **developmental**.

5) Training is done to meet **development** needs.

1) **Hard HRM** can **benefit** a businesses because managers keep **control** of the workforce, so people are less likely to make **mistakes**. Since employees are seen as just another resource, it's easy for the business to **replace** them.

2) Businesses adopting hard HRM **don't** use employees to their **full potential**, so could be **missing out** on chances to increase **profits**. Hard HRM can also be **demotivational** for the workforce. Boring, repetitive jobs can make employees feel **undervalued**. They're unlikely to be loyal to their organisation, leading to **high staff turnover**.

3) **Soft HRM** is likely to increase **staff morale** because employees will feel **valued**. This will make it easier to **retain** staff, and the business will also benefit from the **skills** and **experience** of its staff. It encourages **commitment** and **good performance** from its workers, because they feel loyalty towards the organisation.

4) Soft HRM **isn't** always **appropriate** though — employees might not be interested in **development** or **empowerment**, and soft HRM usually involves more **costs** for businesses because it encourages **investment** in employees. The extra training is also **time-consuming**. There's also a risk that employees who have completed all the training might want to **leave** for a better job.

Practice Questions

Q1 Why is it important to have a diverse workforce?

Q2 How can the HR department help employees reach their full potential?

Q3 What are the external factors that influence HR objectives?

Q4 Why is it important for HR and other departments to work together?

Exam Question

Q1 Explain the difference between hard and soft HRM and analyse the costs and benefits of each. [9 marks]

Soft HRM is always practised in pillow factories...

HRM sounds quite tricky — you've got to make sure you've got the right number of staff who have the right skills and qualifications, then try to stop too many of them from leaving, and try to get them to turn up for work and leave at the end of the day in one piece. Phew. It's definitely a bit easier to learn about it than it is to actually do it...

Interpreting Human Resource Data

A business needs to measure the effectiveness of every resource used, and that includes its employees.
People don't always like the idea of having their performance measured, but it's good for the business.

Human Resource Data is Analysed before making Decisions

1) There are many **figures** that HR consider when making decisions — these include
labour productivity, **labour turnover**, **absenteeism**, **labour retention**, etc.

2) These figures are often calculated using a **performance management system** and are used to
check that the business's human resources are always being used to **maximum efficiency**.

3) HR use this data to **make plans** for the human resource flow in the future (see p.88).

4) They will also compare these figures to their **competitors'** to see who is utilising their **human resources**
better and if they need to **improve** in certain areas. E.g. if **labour retention** rates are **higher** in a competitor's
business, HR need to look at why employees **don't want to stay** at their company.

Labour Productivity affects HR decisions

HR needs to look at **trends** in **labour productivity** figures before making decisions on **training**, **recruitment** and **pay**.

$$\text{Labour Productivity} = \frac{\text{Output per period}}{\text{Number of employees}}$$

See p.58 for more on labour productivity.

1) HR can have a **positive impact** on labour productivity by employing a **diverse** workforce and making sure that
all employees feel **engaged** and **motivated**. They can also make sure the right people are in the **right roles**.
Doing these things will also **reduce levels of absenteeism** which will **increase productivity** even more.

2) If labour productivity is **increasing**, HR might choose to reward employees with **bonuses** and
increased salaries. This will keep levels of **motivation** high and workers know their hard work is **valued**.

3) If labour productivity is **decreasing** then HR might choose to **retrain** staff, offer bigger **incentives** or,
in extreme cases, offer **redundancies** and **replace** employees with more skilled labour.

4) HR will **compare** their labour productivity data to their **competitors'** and see if they need to **improve**,
or if they are already ahead of the game. If productivity is **low** compared to competitors, they might need to
look at how competitors are **managing** their **human resources** — this information is often **tricky** to get hold of.

HR Decisions are affected by lots of Different Performance Statistics

1) Two other important statistics that will affect HR decisions are **labour cost per unit** and
employee costs as a percentage of turnover. They can be calculated using the following formulas:

$$\text{Labour cost per unit} = \frac{\text{Labour costs}}{\text{Units of output}}$$

$$\text{Employee costs as a \% of turnover} = \frac{\text{Employee costs}}{\text{Sales turnover}} \times 100$$

Unless you're told otherwise, assume labour costs are equal to employee costs.

Example: A bread manufacturer has labour costs of £500 000 per year.
They produce 2 000 000 loaves each year and have a turnover of £1 600 000.
Labour cost per unit = £500 000 ÷ 2 000 000 = £0.25 = **25p**
Employee costs as a percentage of turnover = £500 000 ÷ £1 600 000 × 100 = **31.25%**

2) Labour cost per unit shows **how much money** the business has to **pay employees** to make **one unit of output**.

3) Labour cost per unit can be reduced in two ways — by **reducing labour costs** or **increasing labour productivity**.

4) Employee costs as a percentage of turnover show what **percentage** of the money made is spent on **employees**
— this is particularly useful when comparing **different-sized** businesses that make **similar** products.

5) **Controlling** employee costs is a main objective of the HR department — this could mean **increasing** or
decreasing them. E.g. if they **recruit** more employees, employee costs will **increase** but they will look at
labour cost per unit or employee costs as a % of turnover to see the **impact** the recruitment had on the business.

6) Employee costs can be decreased by **reducing wages** and **benefits** — HR will try to avoid this if possible
as it could result in a **demotivated workforce** which could actually make the problem **worse**.

7) HR also needs to think about the **ethics** of the business when making decisions — it might
be more important that staff are **treated well** and feel **valued** even though it will cost a bit more.

Interpreting Human Resource Data

Labour Turnover measures the Proportion of Staff who Leave each year

$$\text{Labour Turnover (\%)} = \frac{\text{Number of staff leaving}}{\text{Average number of staff employed}} \times 100$$

Average number of staff employed = (staff at the beginning of the time period + staff at the end of the time period) ÷ 2.

1) The **higher** the figure, the **larger** the proportion of workers **leaving** the firm each year.

2) **External causes** of high labour turnover include changes in regional **unemployment** levels, and the growth of other local firms using staff with **similar skills**.

3) **Internal causes** of high labour turnover include **poor motivation** of staff, **low wages**, and a lack of opportunities for **promotion**. Staff will **join other firms** to increase their pay and job responsibilities.

4) A **poor recruitment** process which selects incompetent candidates will also increase labour turnover.

5) Increased **delegation**, **job enrichment**, higher **wages** and better **training** can reduce employee turnover.

6) Businesses need **some** labour turnover to bring new ideas in. Labour turnover of 0% means no one **ever** leaves.

Benefits of high staff turnover	Disadvantages of high staff turnover
Constant stream of **new ideas** through new staff.	Lack of **loyal** and **experienced** staff who know the business.
Firm can recruit staff who've **already been trained** by competitors — saves money.	Firm **loses** staff it has **trained**, often to direct competitors.
If sales fall, firm can reduce workforce through **natural wastage** rather than costly redundancy.	**Training costs money** and **productivity drops** while new staff get trained.
Enthusiasm of new staff influences other workers.	**Recruitment** costs are high.

Labour Retention measures a Company's Ability to keep its Employees

$$\text{Labour Retention (\%)} = \frac{\text{Number of staff employed at end of period} - \text{Number of leavers}}{\text{Number of staff employed at end of period}} \times 100$$

1) **Labour retention** is closely related to **labour turnover**. The **higher** the turnover, the **lower** the retention rate.

2) A **low retention rate** means that the company only keeps a **small proportion** of its employees.

3) HR could deal with a **low retention rate** by improving the **induction** process. They could highlight the **opportunities** available to all employees and reinforce the **values** and **goals** of the business so that employees feel **included** and **valued**.

Practice Questions

Q1 Give three ways in which the HR department can help to increase labour productivity.

Q2 A firm produces 50 units per day and its labour cost per unit is £100. What are the firm's daily labour costs?

Answers on p.107.

Q3 State two benefits and two drawbacks of a high labour turnover.

Q4 In 2014, 18 people left a firm which employs an average of 600 staff. Calculate the firm's labour turnover.

Exam Questions

Q1 In 2005 the employee costs as a percentage of turnover of a business was 10%. By 2015 it had risen to 20%. Analyse why this could have happened and suggest ways the HR department could help to decrease it. [9 marks]

Q2 Last year a publishing company had a labour retention rate of 70%. Analyse how the human resource department could help to increase its labour retention. [9 marks]

Hopefully your information retention is at 100%...

All these formulas are quite easy really. Problem is, the numbers alone don't really tell you anything. You need to be able to interpret the figures and apply them to different businesses. E.g. high labour turnover isn't ideal at an aeroplane manufacturer but is totally acceptable at a fast-food restaurant. Now, do you want to go large for an extra £1?

Improving Organisational Design

Hurray, two pages on improving organisational design. It must be your lucky day.

Organisational Design shows Structure and Hierarchy

1) The traditional business structure is a series of levels, where each level has responsibility for, and **authority** over, the levels below. This is called a **hierarchy**, and can be shown on an organisational chart.

2) An **organisational chart** sets out who has **authority** and **responsibility** to make decisions.

3) It shows who individual employees are **accountable** to (who is directly **above** them in the hierarchy) and who employees are **responsible** for (who is directly **below** them in the hierarchy).

4) The chart also shows how the organisation is divided up, e.g. by **department**, by **product** or by **location**.

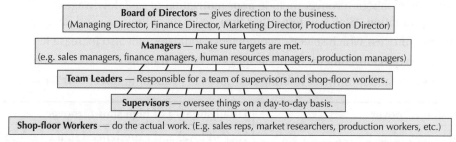

Board of Directors — gives direction to the business.
(Managing Director, Finance Director, Marketing Director, Production Director)

Managers — make sure targets are met.
(e.g. sales managers, finance managers, human resources managers, production managers)

Team Leaders — Responsible for a team of supervisors and shop-floor workers.

Supervisors — oversee things on a day-to-day basis.

Shop-floor Workers — do the actual work. (E.g. sales reps, market researchers, production workers, etc.)

Structures can be Tall or Flat and have wide or narrow Spans of Control

1) Organisations with **lots of levels** in their hierarchy are called "**tall**". Tall structures have long **chains of command**. The chain of command is the path of **communication** and **authority** up and down the hierarchy.

2) Tall structures can affect **communication**. Messages take a **long time** to get from the top to the bottom, or vice-versa. **Decisions** take a long time to make, and there's a lot of **paperwork** to deal with.

3) "**Flat**" organisations only have a few levels in their hierarchy. People are given more **responsibility** and **freedom**.

4) Flat structures can lead to managers getting **overwhelmed** by too many people reporting to them. The **span of control** is the **number of people** who report directly to a manager. Managers in **flat** structures have **wide** spans of control. This means they have a lot of workers answering to them.

5) If the span of control is **too wide**, managers find it hard to manage **effectively**.

6) Managers in tall structures have **narrow** spans of control — they aren't responsible for many people. This allows them to **monitor** the people below them **more closely**.

7) If the span of control is **too narrow**, workers can become **demotivated** — they may feel that they're being **micromanaged** by interfering bosses.

8) It can be hard for a manager to keep a close eye on workers if the span of control is bigger than about 6 people. But if the workers are all doing the **same routine task**, they don't need as much supervision — so a span of control of 10-12 people (or more) is fine.

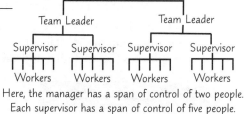

Here, the manager has a span of control of two people.
Each supervisor has a span of control of five people.

Organisational design can be improved through delayering

- Delayering means **removing** parts of the hierarchy — it creates a **flatter** structure with **wider** spans of control.

- Delayering can help to **lower costs**. Cutting management jobs can save a lot of money in salaries. It gives junior employees **enhanced roles** with more responsibility and can improve **communication**.

- It can **cost businesses money** in the short term as the remaining staff need to be **retrained** in their new roles. If you **overdo** it, managers can end up **stressed** and overworked with **huge** spans of control.

Delegation relies on Trust Between the Two Parties

1) Giving responsibility for decision-making to people below you is called **delegation**.

2) The manager needs to **trust** the people they are **delegating** responsibility to. The best managers know the **strengths** and **weaknesses** of the people below them and delegate the right work to the right people.

3) The person being delegated to needs to **trust** that their manager isn't just passing on the work they don't like doing themselves. They should be given **challenging tasks** (to help them develop) as well as **routine tasks**.

4) The amount of delegation is heavily influenced by the **nature** and **culture** of the business — e.g. if the business wants its employees to be loyal and feel valued, it will delegate lots of responsibilities. A business that **delegates** a lot of responsibilities will need to have **many** levels of authority.

Improving Organisational Design

Centralised Structures keep Authority for decisions at the Top

In **centralised** organisations, all decisions are made by **senior managers** at the **top** of the business.

Advantages of centralisation

1) Business leaders have lots of **experience** of making business decisions.

2) Managers get an **overview** of the whole business, so decisions are **consistent** throughout the business.

3) Senior managers **aren't biased** towards one department so they can make the best decisions for the business as a whole.

4) Senior managers can make big decisions **quickly** because they don't have to **consult** anybody else.

Disadvantages of centralisation

1) Not many people are **expert** enough to make decisions about all aspects of the business.

2) **Excluding employees** from decision-making can be **demotivating**.

3) The organisation **reacts slowly** to change, allowing its **competitors** to get ahead. This is because the senior managers who make the decisions don't spend time on the shop floor, so they're slow to notice **consumer trends**.

Decentralised Structures share out the Authority to make decisions

1) Decentralisation **shares out authority** to more **junior** employees.

2) **National** and **multinational** firms **decentralise** decision-making, and **delegate** power to **regional** managers.

3) Managers have to make sure that the **work** of **all** a company's **employees** is **contributing** to the **goals** of the **business**. This can be **difficult** to achieve when a lot of **power** has been **delegated**.

Advantages of decentralisation

1) Involvement in decision-making **motivates employees**.

2) Employees can use **expert knowledge** of their sector.

3) Day-to-day decisions can be made **quickly** without having to ask senior managers.

Disadvantages of decentralisation

1) Junior employees may not have enough **experience** to make decisions.

2) **Inconsistencies** may develop between **divisions** in a business.

3) Junior employees may not be able to see the **overall situation** and needs of an organisation.

The **size**, **nature**, **objectives** and **culture** of a business will all affect whether a centralised or decentralised approach is used — this will then have an impact on the **structure** of the business.

- Businesses might centralise in order to save money in a more competitive market. A **centralised** approach can result in a flat and wide structure as levels of middle management are no longer needed.

- Businesses might **decentralise** as they are **expanding** and operating from a number of different locations. A **decentralised** approach will create more levels of authority and increase the amount of **delegation**.

Practice Questions

Q1 What are the disadvantages of a tall organisational structure?

Q2 Why might a flat structure be popular with junior employees in a business?

Q3 What is meant by "span of control"?

Q4 What's the difference between centralised and decentralised structures?

Exam Questions

Q1 A management consultant has advised Doug McLeod to alter the structure of his business by delayering.
　　a) Complete this sentence. Delayering will make the structure of Doug McLeod's business...
　　　　A Taller and wider　　　B Flatter and narrower　　　C Taller and narrower　　　D Flatter and wider　　[1 mark]
　　b) Discuss the factors that Doug should think about before starting to delayer.　　　　　　　　　[9 marks]

Q2 Evaluate the effectiveness of delegation in centralised and decentralised structures.　　　　　　[12 marks]

Delayering — isn't that taking off your cardigan when it's warm...

It's a shame you can't delegate the learning of your Business course to someone else. But then I guess you'd miss out on the joy of knowing the difference between centralised and decentralised structures and that would be sad...

Managing the Human Resource Flow

The human resource flow is how people move into, out of and within the business.

HR Planning *starts with anticipating* Future Staffing Needs

The **purpose** of human resource planning is to make sure that the business always has the **right number** of staff with the **right skills** to meet its needs. This is done by **predicting** the demand and supply of staff.

1) HR predict **how many** and **what kind** of workers will be **needed** (e.g. **skilled/unskilled, full/part time**).

- HR departments ask other **experienced managers** for their **opinions** and **advice**.
- **Past statistics** are used to see if employee numbers have **risen** or **fallen**.
- An increase or decrease in **demand** for a **product** means an increase or decrease in **need** for **workers**, so the HR department uses the company's sales forecasts to see whether demand for the company's products will rise, fall or stay the same.
- They'll need to decide whether they need **short-term staff** (e.g. if they're recruiting for a seasonal demand) or **long-term staff** (e.g. if they're anticipating growth or a change in production techniques).
- The introduction of **new technology** and **techniques** will alter the number of workers needed.
- HR analyse the **current staff details** to see how many are likely to **leave** or **retire** in the near future. They do an **internal staff stocktake** by looking at the number of employees and their **qualities** and **skills**.

> The workforce should be flexible and adaptable enough to react to a changing environment.

2) HR also needs to assess the potential **supply** of **new workers**:

- They check the **level of unemployment** in the area to find out how many people are looking for work. HR departments see how many **school** and **college leavers** are seeking employment locally.
- **Local infrastructure** is important — good housing, transport and schools can **attract** people to the area. They see if **competitors** are recruiting a similar workforce — if so there'll be **competition** for workers.

Recruitment *can be done* Internally *or* Externally

Identify vacancy → Write person specification and job description → Advertise job → Process applications → Shortlist most suitable candidates → Interview most suitable candidates → Appoint most suitable candidate

1) When they've decided what new staff the business needs, HR draw up a **job description**, including the job title, the main **roles** and **responsibilities** of the job, salary, etc. They also write a **person specification**, detailing the **qualities** and **qualifications** required. HR also decide if they want to **advertise** the job **internally** or **externally**.

	Internal recruitment	External recruitment
Advantages	• Candidates already **know** the business, and the business knows the candidates. • **Short** and **cheap** process. • **Motivates** workers to go for a promotion.	• Brings in fresh **new ideas**. • Brings in **experience** from other organisations. • **Larger** number of applicants.
Disadvantages	• Leaves a **vacancy** in another department. • Can cause **resentment** among colleagues who aren't selected.	• **Long** and **expensive** process. • Candidates will need a **longer** induction process. • Have only seen a candidate at recruitment — might **not** be **representative** of what they're like at work.

2) Sometimes external recruitment will be done using professional **social media** sites such as LinkedIn — this allows businesses to reach a **large** number of people with very **specific** skills.

3) HR also take charge of the **selection procedure** for new staff:

- **Interviews** are the most common way of choosing candidates. Candidates can be interviewed **one-to-one** or by a **panel** of interviewers. Phone interviews are thought to be less effective than **face-to-face** interviews.
- Some organisations use **assessment centres** to help them **test** candidates. Tests include **psychometric** testing which assesses personality fit, **aptitude** tests which find out how good the candidate is at job tasks, and **group exercises** which show how candidates interact with other people in various situations.

4) A good **recruitment process** can help the HR department achieve its **diversity** objectives. They should make sure that they are recruiting workers with a variety of **skills** and from various different **backgrounds**.

5) Internal recruitment also helps to improve **employer/employee relations** as employees feel **motivated** by opportunities to progress in their career.

Managing the Human Resource Flow

HR Plan Employee's *Training* and *Development*

1) HR organises the **induction** and **training** programs of **new** staff.
   They also plan **retraining** and **development** of their current staff.

2) Training and development can be done **off-the-job** (e.g. studying part-time at a local **college**)
   or **on-the-job** (e.g. where the new worker is trained by an experienced worker).

	On-the-job training	Off-the-job training
Advantages	• Easy to **organise**. • **Lower cost** of training. • Training is **job specific**.	• Trainers are **specialists**. • **New ideas** are brought to the business. • **No job distractions** during training.
Disadvantages	• Trainer and trainee are **not productive** during training. • **Bad practices** are passed on. • No **new ideas** are brought to the business.	• Can be **expensive**. • **No benefit** to the business while training. • Training might **not be specific** to their day-to-day job.

3) Managing training correctly can help HR to make employees feel **engaged and involved** —
   it can make workers feel as if the business is **investing** in them and really **values** them.
   If workers feel valued by the business they are also **less likely** to be absent or to leave the company.

4) HR can also develop **specific** training programs to 'fast track' its more talented workers.

HR Flow needs to be *Managed* during the *Tough Times*

1) Some departments might have **too much** labour if there has been
   a recent **drop in demand** or **new technology** has increased efficiency.

2) HR will first see if the surplus staff can be **redeployed** to other areas of the business. This allows the business
   to keep staff **morale** and **motivation** high while also filling other vacancies with staff that they **know** and **trust**.

3) If there is **no way** to redeploy staff then the business will have to make the surplus employees **redundant**.

4) Managing the HR flow in this way can make sure that the business has the **right number** of employees
   and they are being put where the business **needs** them the most.

HR Plans are influenced by *Internal* and *External Factors*

Internal Factors that Influence HR Plans	External Factors that Influence HR Plans
• **Corporate**, **marketing** and **production** plans. E.g. if production is expanding they will need to recruit more staff and offer more training. • Changes in **production style** may lead to retraining, recruitment or redeployment of staff.	• **Employment legislation** protects employees' rights and **restricts** companies' ability to dismiss or transfer workers. • **New technology** might change the **number** of staff and the **skills** needed — businesses might have to **retrain** their staff. • **Labour market trends** like **migration** and the **ageing population** have an effect on the **supply** of workers.

Practice Questions

Q1 What factors do HR consider when trying to predict a firm's future staffing needs?

Q2 Give two advantages of on-the-job training and off-the-job training.

Q3 Explain how external factors can impact HR plans.

Exam Questions

Q1 Evaluate the advantages and disadvantages of internal and external
   recruitment for a retail organisation with 200 stores nationwide. [12 marks]

Q2 The HR department of an expanding business is carrying out a major HR planning exercise.
   Analyse how they could recruit, train and redeploy staff to match the business's new objectives. [9 marks]

Always be nice to HR staff, your future is in their hands...

Human resource planning is all about predicting what's going to happen in the future. Sometimes you get it right, and everything goes along swimmingly. Other times you get it wrong, and end up paying people to twiddle their thumbs.

Motivation and Job Design

For the past 150 years, industrial psychologists and sociologists have tried to figure out what motivates workers...

Motivated Employees get More Done than Non-motivated Employees

1) The value of motivation should not be **underestimated** — a motivated workforce is likely to be more **productive**, more aligned with **company objectives** and prepared to go **above and beyond** for the company.

2) Motivated workers are more **loyal**, which will decrease both **labour turnover** and **absences**, which reduces costs.

3) **Customer satisfaction** usually increases when a workforce feel **engaged** with what they are doing.

4) A company that **motivates** and **engages** its employees is a more attractive prospect for **future employees**. Companies with a **good reputation** will attract the **best employees** and gain a **competitive advantage**.

5) There are several different **motivational theories** — they each suggest different ways to motivate employees.

1) Taylor and Scientific Management — Concentrate on Efficiency

1) In the early 20th century, F.W. Taylor thought that workers were motivated by **money**. He believed workers would do the **minimum** amount of work if left to their own devices.

2) Taylor's goal was to figure out the **most efficient** way to do a job, and then make sure every single worker did it that way. Also, making sure that each task was being done by the **right worker**. This approach is called **scientific management**.

3) He favoured **division of labour** — breaking work down into a lot of **small repetitive tasks**, with managers taking **responsibility** for the workforce.

4) Taylor believed in paying workers according to the **quantity** they produced — the most **productive** workers got a **better rate**. He believed that financial incentives would **motivate** workers and raise **productivity**.

5) Increased productivity meant that **fewer workers** were needed — workers worried about losing their jobs.

6) There were other disadvantages, too — increased productivity could lead to a reduction in **quality**. **Supervisors** were needed to monitor efficiency and for quality control purposes.

Taylor's approach wouldn't work for modern businesses — it would be seen as **exploitation**. It also ignores the **demotivating** effect of doing very repetitive boring work. However, aspects of Taylor's theory have survived — **piece rate pay** is based on his ideas, and the **supervisor role** still exists.

2) Maslow's Hierarchy of Needs — people need the Basics

Maslow said that people start by meeting the needs at the **bottom** of the pyramid. Once they've sorted out those needs, they can move on to the needs on the **next level** up.

Maslow and Herzberg both believed that workers had needs which were specific to them as individuals.

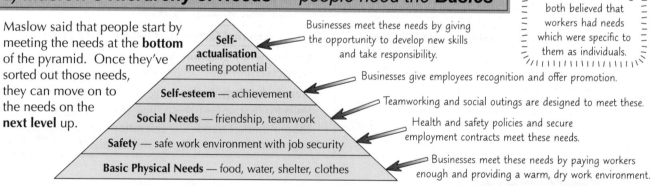

Businesses meet these needs by giving the opportunity to develop new skills and take responsibility.

Self-actualisation meeting potential

Businesses give employees recognition and offer promotion.

Self-esteem — achievement

Teamworking and social outings are designed to meet these.

Social Needs — friendship, teamwork

Health and safety policies and secure employment contracts meet these needs.

Safety — safe work environment with job security

Basic Physical Needs — food, water, shelter, clothes

Businesses meet these needs by paying workers enough and providing a warm, dry work environment.

Maslow's theory is **appealing** as each of the five different needs have some **importance** to workers. However, it isn't always **obvious** which level an **individual** is at. Different workers may put their needs in a **different order**, e.g. some may value friendship and teamwork over achievement and meeting potential.

3) Herzberg's Hygiene and Motivating factors

In the 1950s and '60s, Frederick Herzberg interviewed accountants and engineers to find out what **motivated** and **satisfied** them at work. He identified **two groups of factors** which influenced the motivation of workers:

1) **Hygiene factors** are things like good **company policy, supervision, working conditions, pay,** and **relations** with fellow employees. They don't motivate as such, but if they **aren't good**, workers get **dissatisfied**.

2) **Motivating factors** are things like **interesting work**, personal **achievement**, **recognition** of achievement, and scope for more **responsibility** and personal **development**. These factors **do** positively motivate workers.

Herzberg's theory recognises that motivation comes from the **individuals' needs** and has influenced **motivational techniques** today — it provides clear solutions for businesses. However, it is often criticised for being based on a **small sample** of people and it doesn't consider that people have **different** hygiene and motivation needs.

Motivation and Job Design

Job Design outlines the way a job is Planned and Organised

1) **Job design** sets out the details of **what** is to be done and **how** it is to be done. It's **influenced** by **internal** and **external factors** that affect how the job can be carried out **effectively**.

2) The **day-to-day** tasks are the main **influence** on the **job design**. The things that need to be considered are: the **range** and **nature** of the tasks, the **way** and **order** tasks need to be completed, the **speed** the tasks need to be done, the **quality** required and the **number of people** required to complete the task.

3) External factors such as **new technology**, changes to **law** and **legislation**, **customer demand** and the availability of certain **skills** can all affect job design.

Hackman and Oldham — Job Design is Focused on the Person not the Job

1) **Taylor's scientific management** approach focused on **how** the job was done, whereas **Maslow's** and **Herzberg's** theories said that **more than money** was needed to motivate workers.

2) **Hackman** and **Oldham** thought that a job needed to be **designed** so that it would focus on the **person**, and the person would then be **motivated**.

3) Hackman and Oldham's model is broken down into **five key elements** of job design which lead to worker **motivation**, more worker **involvement**, higher **performance**, lower **staff turnover** and lower **absenteeism**.

Job Characteristic	Impact of the characteristic on the workers	Effect on the workers
Skill variety Task identity Task significance	Makes work more meaningful for the workers	Motivation is improved Workers feel involved
Autonomy	Workers have more responsibility	Quality of work is improved Workers are more satisfied
Feedback	Workers know how well they are performing and aim to improve	with their work and are more committed to the business

Autonomy means giving workers the freedom to make their own decisions.

- **Skill variety** — A wide variety of skills needed in a job can **motivate**. A lack of skill variety can demotivate.
- **Task identity** — Workers will feel **involved** if there is a clear task and they deal with it from start to finish.
- **Task significance** — If people think the job they are doing is **significant**, they will be motivated to do it well.
- **Autonomy** — Workers who make their **own decisions** will feel like their contribution is valued.
- **Feedback** — This tells the workers how they have **performed** and encourages them to do better.

4) Job design should constantly be adapted to meet the needs of the **business** and the **individuals**.

5) **Changing** job design has an **immediate** impact on **HR objectives**, as employees feel **engaged** and **involved**.

6) It can also have a less immediate effect on the overall **corporate objectives**, e.g. it can help to reduce the **costs** of the business, improve **productivity** of the workforce and improve **quality** of the product.

Practice Questions

Q1 Give three benefits of a motivated workforce.
Q2 Give a brief description of Taylor's views on motivation.
Q3 Give five factors that Herzberg would describe as 'hygiene factors'.
Q4 Write and describe the five job characteristics in the Hackman and Oldham model.

Exam Questions

Q1 Cheapos is a local supermarket chain that has a reputation for poor customer service. Analyse, with reference to Maslow's hierarchy, how Cheapos could motivate its workers to improve their customer service. [9 marks]

Q2 Use the Hackman and Oldham model to explain the effect of good job design on workers. [6 marks]

Design me a job where I sit and eat biscuits all day and I'm there...

Make sure you know the theories of motivation — the ideas might well come in handy for giving examples of how managers today can increase the motivation of their workers. You'll need to know about job design too.

Improving Motivation

Some businesses motivate their employees by offering financial incentives, others motivate their workers using non-financial methods. Personally I'm motivated by the thought of cheese and biscuits at the end of the day...

Payment Methods can be used to Reward and Motivate

There are several different ways a business can **pay** its employees:

Piece rate	Workers are paid per **unit produced**. They **don't** get a fixed salary and **aren't entitled** to sick pay, holiday pay or company pensions.
Salary Schemes	Workers are paid according to a given **time period**. This could be an **hourly rate**, a **weekly wage** or an **annual wage**.
Commission	Workers are paid a **bonus** on top of their salary — the bonus could be based on **sales** or **units produced**.
Performance-related pay	Workers are paid based on their **performance** or on the performance of the business. The amount is determined by both the **individual** and the **business meeting targets** — this is often done in annual **appraisals**.

1) **Piece rate** is used when the **quantity** produced can be measured easily — it can motivate workers to produce a **high quantity** of products. However, **quality** and **morale** can **suffer** and the manager will need to make sure some **quality control** measures are put in place. This is often used for **production/assembly line** workers.

2) Employees on **salary schemes** have to work a **minimum** number of hours and produce a certain amount of work. If they **don't** do the amount of work required, they will be expected to **work longer** until it is finished. This can **motivate** workers to do work quickly while not compromising on quality. The downside of salary schemes is that workers **can't** earn extra money by **working harder** and producing better **quality work**.

3) **Commission** is often used in **sales roles** such as in clothing stores and at car dealerships — workers are **rewarded** for selling certain products. It can increase **motivation** and **performance** of sales staff. However, it can also lead to **overselling**, and customers can feel like they are **overwhelmed** by staff whenever they enter the store. The business also doesn't know how much its **labour costs** will be each month.

4) **Performance-related pay** can be used to reward your **best workers**. Workers are motivated to meet their own **targets** and ensure the business meets its **objectives** — however, it can lead to **demoralisation** of staff if only certain people are getting increased pay when the **whole business** is doing well.

5) Employees may also get **fringe benefits**. These can include a **staff discount** for company products (common in retail, not so common in aircraft manufacturing...), employer contributions to employee **pensions**, private **medical insurance**, a company **car**, **profit-sharing** schemes or **shares** in the company.

Flexible Working can help to motivate Employees

1) Flexible working is when **working hours** and **patterns** are adapted to suit the **employees**.

2) Businesses offering flexible working are an **attractive prospect** to **highly skilled workers**. There are several types of flexible working, including:

- **Flexi-time** — employees work **full-time hours**, but they can **decide** when to work, around fixed **core hours**. E.g. employees might have to work for 37 hours a week, but they only have to be in the office Mon-Fri between the hours of 10 am and 3 pm — the rest of their hours can be made up any time they like.
- **Compressed hours** — employees work a set number of **hours** per week, but over **fewer days**.
- **Annual hours** — employees work a certain number of **hours** over the **year**, but they choose when to work. E.g. employees with children might not work as much in the school holidays.
- **Job-sharing** — **two people** share **one job**, e.g. working alternate weeks or splitting the week between them.
- **Home working** — employees work from **home** instead of at the business premises.

Advantages of flexible working	Disadvantages of flexible working
1) Flexible working improves **motivation** so employee **productivity** should improve.	1) It can be impractical for businesses that need to serve the **public** during normal working hours.
2) Flexible working helps employees with **children**.	2) Home-workers may be easily **distracted** at home.
3) Home working suits **families**, **disabled** workers and those who live in **remote** places.	3) Job-sharing can lead to **confusion** over responsibilities and **unequal** workloads.

Improving Motivation

Non-Financial Motivation — Jobs are Designed to be more Satisfying

Lots of businesses today **design jobs** to be **motivating** (see p.90-91). There are **different ways** to do this:

1) **Job enlargement** gives the employee **more work** at the same level.

2) **Job enrichment** gives workers more **challenging** work, and the **training** they need to do it. It gives employees more **responsibility** for organising their work and solving problems.

See p.63 for more on quality circles.

3) **Empowerment** gives people **control** over their work, and a greater role in **decision-making** — **quality circles** let groups of workers from various departments meet to suggest **improvements** to productivity and quality.

4) **Teamworking** puts workers into **small teams** and lets them **organise** their own work — this can lead to **job enrichment** and **empowerment** as workers get a greater role in a variety of tasks.

5) Businesses can also motivate their employees by creating a **pleasant** working environment or providing **facilities** for the workers to use (e.g. free gym/sports facilities). These things can make workers feel as if the business is looking after them and will **motivate** the workers to do their **best work** for the business.

Organisational and Job Design affect the type of Motivation

1) **Organisational design** (see p.86) will influence the type of **payment method** a company chooses. E.g. a company with a **tall** structure might be more inclined to use piece rate or performance-related pay because there are lots of levels of authority to monitor the productivity and progress of the people below them.

2) The **size** of the business will also influence the payment methods chosen. E.g. a national supermarket chain might pay its shopfloor staff an **hourly rate** as it is difficult to distinguish one person's work from another.

3) Organisational design can also affect the non-financial motivation a company chooses. A business with a **flat** structure might **not** want to introduce **teamworking**, because **team leaders** introduce an **extra** level of **hierarchy**. They might try to motivate people through job **enlargement** or **enrichment** instead.

4) **Empowerment** is common in businesses with flat structures as **communication** is easier — this leads to staff feeling more motivated as they are being included in **decision-making**.

5) Businesses with **large numbers** of highly-skilled workers might put greater emphasis on non-financial motivation. **Highly-skilled workers** are more likely to respond to things like job **enrichment** and **empowerment** than they are to respond to financial incentives.

6) Non-financial incentives are a **long term** type of motivation — a company and its management invest a lot of time, money and effort into getting it right. If a business needs a job done **quickly** then it is much more likely to focus on **financial** incentives.

Practice Questions

Q1 Define the terms 'piece rate', 'commission', 'salary schemes' and 'performance-related pay'.

Q2 List three advantages and three disadvantages of flexible working.

Q3 Explain what is meant by the terms 'job enrichment' and 'job enlargement'.

Q4 Give five non-financial motivation techniques that businesses use.

Q5 Give a way in which the design of a business will affect the payment methods used.

Exam Questions

Q1 Colin is a checkout clerk in a supermarket, Jane is a travelling sales representative and Mike is a bricklayer. Say whether each person is likely to be paid by piece rate, hourly rate or commission, and explain why. [6 marks]

Q2 Analyse the effects of organisational design and job design on the type of motivation a business uses. [9 marks]

Q3 Analyse how the financial incentives of a multinational corporation might change as you move up the hierarchy. [9 marks]

Sadly I don't get paid on commission for all these gags...

Believe it or not, people aren't just in it for the money! Shocking, I know, but businesses also need to offer their workers some sort of non-financial motivation. Getting the balance right is what all businesses strive to achieve....

Improving Employer-Employee Relations

Communication is really important in business. I bet you never would've guessed that...

Employers and Employees need to Cooperate with each other

1) Employers and employees **need each other**. **Employers** need **hard-working staff** to contribute to the production of goods or a service that can be sold for a profit. **Employees** need a **secure income** to support themselves and their families.

2) However, there can be **conflict** between them. Employers would prefer to pay **lower wages** to keep **costs** down but employees want **higher wages** to improve their **standard of living**.

The two sides must **negotiate** to reach an **acceptable compromise** on wage rates, working conditions and terms of employment. **Failure** to reach agreement could lead to a **production stoppage**, and **both parties** would **suffer**.

A **successful** employer-employee relationship **maximises** the **cooperation** and **minimises** the potential for **conflict** between these two groups. It is built on a **culture of trust** between the two groups.

Communication between Managers and Employees is Essential

1) The purpose of communication is to pass on **information** and **ideas**.

2) Communication **within** the business is necessary for making **plans**, giving **instructions** and **motivating** staff. Managers need to communicate **goals** and **objectives** to staff so they know what they're meant to be aiming for.

3) For communication to be effective, the message that's **received** should be the **same** as the message that was **sent**.

4) Good communication is **clear** and **unambiguous**. If a manager arranges a conference call to start at 6 am but half the people who are suppose to be in the call think it starts at 6 pm, communication has obviously failed.

5) Effective communication is a **two-way thing**. Managers have to tell employees what they want them to **know**, and they also need to **listen** to what their employees have to say to them — employees will offer **new ideas** from a different **point of view**.

6) Good communication and relations make it easier for employees to accept **difficult decisions**. It can also help the **feedback** and **complaints** processes to run more smoothly.

Organisations need to Overcome Barriers to Improve Communication

There are several **barriers** that can prevent communication from being **effective**:

Attitudes — The receiver may **dislike** the sender or the receiver may be distracted.

Intermediaries — The **longer** the chain of communication, the more **mangled** the message becomes.

Language barriers — One word can mean **different things** in different cultures. **Jargon** can be confusing.

Sense of purpose — Staff who **don't understand why** they're being told something may ignore future messages.

Communication overload — If employees are **swamped** with messages, they won't be able to deal with them all.

Remoteness — It's easy to **misinterpret** the tone when you can't hear the speaker's voice (e.g. in letters or emails).

Group behaviour — Some employees might be **overbearing**, making others too **afraid** to speak up in meetings.

These barriers can be overcome by creating a **trusting relationship** between employers and employees.

1) Creating a more **democratic** management style allows everyone in the business to have a say in how things are run. This means that decisions are made when the **majority** of employees and employers agree on an issue. This **inclusiveness** makes employees feel more valued.

2) Making sure both parties recognise each others' **objectives** and **needs** can stop employees being told things they don't need to know or don't care about. It can **prevent** both parties feeling **overloaded** with information and **improve attitudes** within the business.

3) Changing **organisational structure** can help to reduce the number of intermediaries — **delayering** (see p.86) is a way in which businesses try to do this. A **flatter** organisational structure can help employees be more **involved** in decisions.

4) **Delegation** and **decentralisation** can also lead to more effective communication. **Empowering** employees can help reduce **negative** attitudes, give employees a **sense of purpose**, reduce a feeling of **remoteness** and eliminate **group behaviour**.

Betty soon began to regret telling her boss she was fluent in Japanese.

Improving Employer-Employee Relations

Good Employer-Employee Relations can Benefit Both Parties

1) Businesses with **good** employer-employee relations will get **more** from their employees than businesses with **poor relations**. Employees will also benefit from **maintaining** a good relationship with their employer.

Benefits to the employer	Benefits to the employee
The business will develop a **great reputation** among **prospective** employees, so it will attract the very best candidates during **recruitment**.	Employees will feel **involved** in the business which will give them a sense of **job security**.
If relations are good then **productivity** and **efficiency** are increased as new ideas and ways of working are picked up **quickly** by the employees. This allows the business to be more **competitive**.	If workers are more **productive** and **efficient** then the business will make **more money**. This increase in profit can be fed back into the workforce through **bonuses** or **pay increases**.
Getting the point of view of the employee is beneficial in making decisions. More **diverse** opinions will mean the business makes more **informed** decisions.	The **views** of the employee are considered during **decisions** so they will feel valued and motivated. This will increase their **job satisfaction**.
Good **communication** will mean that the objectives of the **employees** are more aligned with the objectives of the **business**.	Employees are able to communicate their **personal objectives** to the employer, which will help the employee **develop skills** and further their career.

2) **Employers** have to be careful not to have **too close** a relationship with their employees. Managers need to be able to keep some **control** over what's going on.

3) **Employers** need to make sure that they **aren't** employing workers just because they have a good relationship with them. They should expect the same **high standards** from every employee regardless of their relationship.

Each Employee has an Individual Relationship with their Employer

1) All employees of a company are treated as **individuals** for some purposes, such as employee appraisals. When **individual employees** negotiate with their employer about their own **working conditions**, it's known as **individual bargaining**.

2) **Individual bargaining** for **pay** means that employers can decide to pay an employee what they think he or she is **worth** to the firm. It might be **more** or **less** than other employees in the same role. This provides a financial **incentive** to the employee to work productively.

3) **Individual bargaining** is also used for things like **flexible working arrangements** — they're often based on the employee's **personal circumstances**, e.g. if an employee cares for young children or an elderly parent, the employer might allow that employee to work from home or work flexi-time (see p.92).

Practice Questions

Q1 Why is efficient communication between managers and employees essential?
Q2 Give seven barriers that can prevent communication being effective.
Q3 Give three benefits to the employer of a good employer-employee relationship.

Exam Questions

Q1 A publishing company is nationally considered to have a great relationship with its employees. Explain why this would make the business an attractive prospect for a prospective candidate. [6 marks]

Q2 Jenson & Hamilton Housing is a national estate agent. Discuss the barriers to communication that the estate agent could face and outline a plan that the business could use to overcome these barriers. [12 marks]

Employer-employee relations aren't just found in family businesses...

Good communication is incredibly important in business. Managers and staff have to communicate with each other to get the job done properly. The better the employer-employee relationship is, the easier communication will be.

Employee Representation

Obviously all businesses like their employees to do some work, but some like them to get more involved...

Employees can be Represented in the Decision Making Process

All businesses need ways of **communicating** with their workforce. They also need a way to **represent** the workforce in the decision-making process. The way that workers are represented will depend on many factors:

- **Organisational size** — in small businesses, employees can talk **directly** to managers about business decisions. In larger companies, employees need a **representative** to give them a **voice** at a higher level.
- **Organisational structure** — in wide and flat structures employees' views are **more likely** to be represented. In narrow and tall structures, communication can be **poor** and employees are **less likely** to be represented.
- **Leadership** and **management** — some businesses have a very **democratic** management style and so employee representation is **encouraged**. However some businesses (usually those adopting **hard HRM** — see p.83), do not like their employees to be involved in the decision-making process.
- **External factors** — the state of the **economy** can impact the extent to which employees are involved in decisions, e.g. in a **recession** the views of the employees might not be represented as the business is just trying to survive. **Legislation** can also dictate the extent to which employees are represented.

Works Councils discuss Work Issues

1) **Works councils** are committees made up of **employer** and **employee** representatives (usually elected).
2) They **meet regularly** to discuss **general work issues** e.g. training, new technology and methods of work.
3) The sharing of ideas and information in a relatively **relaxed** atmosphere does a lot to improve **relations**.
4) **Quality circles** (see p.63) are like works councils, but they only discuss **quality** issues. They meet regularly to discuss ways of improving quality. Quality circles include employees from **all levels** of the business.
5) In 1994, the EU brought in **European Works Councils** for businesses based in multiple European countries.

Trade Unions Negotiate with Employers on behalf of Employees

1) **Trade unions** act on behalf of **groups of employees** in the workforce when negotiating rates of **pay** and **working conditions** etc. with the employer.
2) By joining with others and belonging to a union, an employee **strengthens** their **bargaining power** in a way that wouldn't be possible if they tried to bargain as an **individual**.
3) Trade unions allow employers and workers to **communicate** with each other.
4) Trade unions give **advice** and **assistance** to **individual** employees who are having problems with their employer.

Trade unions take action in the workplace

1) Trade unions **negotiate** with employers on behalf of their members to secure fair rates of pay and/or productivity bonuses for their work.
2) Trade unions help negotiate reasonable **hours of work**, and **paid holiday** entitlement.
3) Trade unions help members get **safe** and civilized **working conditions**.
4) Trade unions help their members get greater **job security** with protection against **mistreatment**, **discrimination** and **unfair dismissal**.

If these negotiations don't work, trade unions may encourage workers to go on strike.

Trade unions take action at a national level

1) Trade unions can **put pressure on the Government** to bring in legislation that will serve the interests of the trade union members.
2) The **minimum wage** was introduced in **1998** by the Government after discussions with trade unions.
3) Trade unions pushed the Government to make **redundancy payments** compulsory.
4) Following demands from trade unions, the **Pension Protection Fund** was set up in April 2005 to protect the pensions of employees in private company pension schemes if their employer **goes bust**.

Trade unions take action in party politics

1) Many unions donate money to the **Labour Party** because they think its policies represent their interests.
2) In the 1970s and 80s, unions had a lot of **power** in the Labour Party. Since the **90s** they've had **less power**.

Employee Representation

Trade Unions can influence the Decisions of the Business

1) When employers want to make **changes** to the **working practices** of the business (e.g. if the employer wants to reduce employees' contracted hours, or change the way it pays staff from an hourly wage to a piece rate, or vice versa), trade unions can help staff if they want to **resist** the change, e.g. by organising **strikes**.

2) Trade unions can also **facilitate change** by **liaising** between employers and union members, and communicating the **benefits** of the change in working practices to their members.

3) **Employees** are more likely to be **open** to change if union representatives are involved in decisions, because they **trust** trade unions to protect their interests, but may **not** trust their employers to do the same.

4) Trade unions stand up for employees' rights if employers want to make **redundancies**. They can negotiate with employers to persuade them to make **fewer** employees redundant, or negotiate better **redundancy payouts**.

5) If employers are planning changes that might **adversely affect** the current workforce, trade unions try to **prevent** these changes from taking place. E.g. if employers want to take on **cheaper** staff, current employees' wages could be **driven down**. A trade union would try to **stop** the recruitment of cheaper workers from going ahead.

6) If current staff are **overworked**, trade unions can try to convince employers to take on **more staff**.

7) Employers can **benefit** from trade unions too — if the business is **profitable**, its good news for **both** the employers and the employees, so it's in the interests of the trade unions to help the business achieve its objectives.

8) Trade union reps can share their **knowledge** about **employment law**, **health and safety**, etc. with the employer.

Employee Representation has Advantages and Disadvantages

Employers and employees need to **cooperate** with each other to maintain a successful working relationship.

Advantages of employee representation	Disadvantages of employee representation
1) It's often more **effective** to approach an organisation as a group. Groups have a bigger **influence** and can be more **forceful**.	1) Employee representation can lead to **industrial action**. This can take the form of deliberately decreased **productivity** or **strike** action.
2) **Collective bargaining** can help achieve **long-term aims** because employers may sign **contracts** which lock them into **agreements**.	2) Strike action can **get out of hand** or turn **violent**.
3) It can be helpful for management to have a **small representative group** of workers to negotiate with rather than consulting every individual.	3) Industrial action leads to **lost profits**.
	4) The majority vote within a trade union may **overrule** the demands of the individual. The individual is then **denied** the **opportunity** to represent themselves as they might want to.
4) Senior management get a **direct insight** into the concerns of the workforce.	5) Industrial action can **undermine the trust** between employer and employee. A **breakdown** in communication will damage the **relationship**.

Practice Questions

Q1 What is a works council?

Q2 What do trade unions do for their members?

Q3 Give two examples of ways that trade unions have influenced Government policy.

Q4 How can unions influence employment levels in a company?

Q5 Give three disadvantages of employee representation.

Exam Questions

Q1 Snapdragon Ltd. is a medium-sized clothes retailer employing 600 people in 10 stores across the country. Discuss the advantages and disadvantages to the employer of its staff being trade union members. [6 marks]

Q2 Sarah works at a large company with a tall and narrow structure. She is not a member of a trade union. Evaluate how Sarah could best raise concerns with her employers. [12 marks]

Trade unions be representin' the employees, yo...

You have to know how employee representation is done, why it's good, and what problems can arise from it. You also should learn the influences employee representation has on the decision making of a business.

Maths Skills

There are loads of statistics involved in running a business, so you need to be able to understand what they all mean.

Businesses produce lots of Statistics

1) Businesses have a lot of **figures** — e.g. figures for sales, costs, revenues and profit, and market research data.

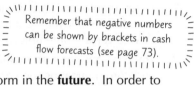
Remember that negative numbers can be shown by brackets in cash flow forecasts (see page 73).

2) Businesses need to understand what their figures **mean** so that they know how well the business is **performing**, and can forecast how well it will perform in the **future**. In order to understand the data and be able to use it, they present it in a way that makes it **easy** to understand.

Diagrams make data Easier to Understand

1) **Pie charts** can be used to show **market share**. Each **1% share** is represented by a **3.6°** section of the pie (because there's 360° in a circle and 360 ÷ 100 = 3.6). Pie charts are **simple to use** and **easy** to **understand**. They can be created quickly using **spreadsheets**.

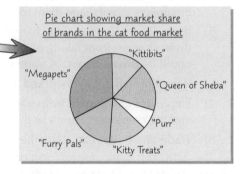
Pie chart showing market share of brands in the cat food market
"Kittibits" — "Queen of Sheba" — "Purr" — "Kitty Treats" — "Furry Pals" — "Megapets"

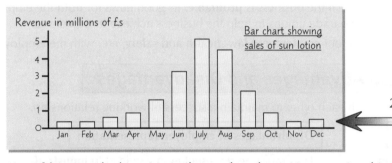
Revenue in millions of £s
Bar chart showing sales of sun lotion
Jan Feb Mar Apr May Jun July Aug Sep Oct Nov Dec

2) **Bar charts** show different values for a **single variable**. They're **easy** to **construct**, easy to **interpret** and they have **high visual impact**.

3) A **histogram** looks quite similar to a bar chart. However, in a histogram the **area** of each block is proportional to the value of the variable measured (not just the height), and there are no gaps between the blocks. So a histogram is different from a bar chart because the bars can vary in both **width** and **height**. Histograms are suitable for comparing variables with **large ranges**.

4) A **pictogram** is a bar chart or histogram where the bars are **pictures** — logos or images. Pictograms are often used in **corporate brochures** — e.g. Cadbury might use pictures of their choccie bars in their sales charts.

5) **Line graphs** plot one variable against another — e.g. sales against time (see p.32). **More than one line** can be shown to make comparisons — they should be in different colours to keep the graph easy to read.

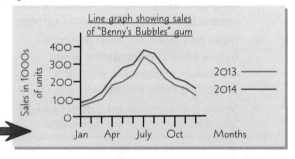
Line graph showing sales of "Benny's Bubbles" gum
Sales in 1000s of units
Jan Apr July Oct   Months
2013   2014

Diagrams can be Misleading

1) Graphs and charts can sometimes give a **false impression** of what is actually going on.

2) If the scales on a graph don't start at **zero**, it can be difficult to see what they show and the meaning can be distorted — e.g. the graph on the right seems to show that the profit has **tripled** between 2010 and 2013, but actually it has only gone up by **10%**.

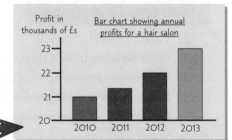
Profit in thousands of £s
Bar chart showing annual profits for a hair salon
2010 2011 2012 2013

You need to be able to Analyse Data and Graphs

- As well as being able to read graphs and charts, you need to be able to **analyse** them.
- This means you need to be able to say what you think is the **important bit** of the chart — e.g. an upward trend in sales, or a big market share.
- You need to be able to say what you think is **causing** it, and what the potential **effects** might be — e.g. a **decrease** in market share might have been caused by the arrival of a new **competitor**, so the **marketing** budget will have to be **increased** to try to get the market share back.

Maths Skills

Data is clustered around an *Average* — *Mean*, *Median* or *Mode*

1) The **mean** is found by **adding together** all numbers in a data set and **dividing** the total by the **number of values** in the data set. Shops could calculate the mean spend per customer:

> **Example:** 5 customers spend £5.90, £27.97, £13.62, £24.95 and £78.81
>
> $$\text{Mean spend} = \frac{5.9 + 27.97 + 13.62 + 24.95 + 78.81}{5} = \frac{151.25}{5} = £30.25$$

2) The **median** is the **middle** value in a data set once all the values are put in **ascending order** — e.g. a business might rank all salespeople by the revenue they've generated over the past month, then identify the **median** and pay everyone above this position a bonus for good performance.

3) The **mode** is the **most common number** in a data set. E.g. Marks & Spencer might check the modal dress size when planning their shop displays so that the mannequins would reflect the most common body size among British women.

4) The **range** is the **difference** between the **largest** and the **smallest** in a group of numbers. It's not an average, but it's often used alongside averages.

5) A **confidence interval** is a range of values used to show the **uncertainty** of an **estimate**. E.g. if a business estimates sales of 2200 units, they might say that they are **95% confident** that the actual sales will be **between** 2000 and 2400. Luckily you don't have to calculate confidence intervals, you just need to know what they mean.

Confidence intervals are on p.34.

Index Numbers show Changes in data over time

1) **Index numbers** are a simple way of showing percentage changes in a set of data over time.

2) Businesses take a set of data showing revenue/profits etc. over a number of years, and make the earliest year the **base year** — the value for the base year is set as 100, and the figures for the following years are shown as a **percentage** of this figure. E.g. the table below shows the index numbers for revenue for an Italian restaurant:

Year	Total Revenue	Revenue Index (2010 = 100)
2010	£17 000	100
2011	£19 550	115
2012	£21 250	125
2013	£22 440	132
2014	£24 650	145

To work out the revenue index for any year, take the total revenue from that year, divide it by the total revenue in the base year and multiply it by 100, e.g. for 2013:

$$\frac{22\,440}{17\,000} \times 100 = 132$$

3) The main advantage of indexing is that it makes it easy to see trends within the business.

Rearrange Formulas to get them into the Form you Want

Sometimes you'll have to **rearrange** a formula before you put the numbers in. Rearrange so that the value you're trying to find is on one side of the formula, and everything else is on the other side.

> **Example:** A company selling novelty doorbells has fixed costs of £6000 and the variable cost per unit is £15. They have to sell 1500 units to break even. What is the selling price per unit?
>
> Use the formula: **Contribution per unit = selling price per unit − variable costs per unit**
> Rearrange to get the value you're looking for on its own:
> **Selling price per unit = contribution per unit + variable costs per unit**
>
> *See p.78 for a reminder of the break-even formulas.*
>
> But you don't know the contribution per unit, so you'll need another formula to work this out:
>
> $$\text{Break-even output} = \frac{\text{fixed costs}}{\text{contribution per unit}}$$
>
> Rearrange to get contribution per unit on its own: $\text{Contribution per unit} = \dfrac{\text{fixed costs}}{\text{break-even output}}$
>
> So: $\text{Selling price per unit} = \dfrac{\text{fixed costs}}{\text{break-even output}} + \text{variable costs per unit}$
>
> $$= \frac{6000}{1500} + 15 = 4 + 15 = \mathbf{19}. \qquad \text{So each novelty doorbell must sell for } \mathbf{£19}.$$

Maths Skills

Businesses use **Percentage Changes** to **Analyse** Figures

1) Businesses work out **percentage** increases or decreases in figures like sales volume, revenue, profit and market share in order to see how performance is **progressing** over time. By looking at percentage changes over a number of months or years, they can see **trends** in the business's performance.

2) The **formula** for working out percentage change is:

$$\text{Percentage change} = \frac{\text{new figure} - \text{previous figure}}{\text{previous figure}} \times 100$$

E.g. if sales of hats have gone up from 9000 to 11 000,
the percentage increase in sales is (11 000 – 9000) ÷ 9000 × 100 = 22.2%.

3) By rearranging the formula, you can **increase a figure** by a **percentage**:

$$\text{New figure} = \frac{\text{percentage change} \times \text{previous figure}}{100} + \text{previous figure}$$

E.g. if a business's profit was £40 000 in 2013 and it increased by 20% in 2014,
then the 2014 profit was (20 × 40 000) ÷ 100 + 40 000 = 8000 + 40 000 = £48 000.

Percentages, **Fractions** and **Ratios** are all **Related**

Related: 100 percentages that
will restore your faith in humanity
(#148 BLEW MY MIND)

You could be given data about a company or a product in a few different ways, and you should be able to convert between them.

To get from **fractions to percentages**, times by 100. And to get from **percentages to fractions**, divide by 100 and simplify.

For example, if $\frac{1}{4}$ of a company's total revenue is profit, then $\frac{1}{4} \times 100 = \mathbf{25\%}$ of its total revenue is profit.

You can also convert from **fractions to ratios** — a ratio is a way of comparing one amount to another. Here, there is 1 part profit to 4 parts revenue, so the ratio of **total revenue to profit** is 4:1. This means that for every £4 of revenue, the company makes £1 of profit.

> **Example:** During one year, the average number of employees at a company is 100, and 20 employees leave the company. Calculate the labour turnover as a percentage and as a fraction, and find the ratio of the number of employees leaving to the average number of employees.
>
> $$\text{Labour Turnover (\%)} = \frac{\text{Number of staff leaving}}{\text{Average number of staff employed}} \times 100$$
>
> *See page 85 for more on labour turnover.*
>
> $\text{Labour Turnover (\%)} = \frac{20}{100} \times 100 = \mathbf{20\%}$, so labour turnover as a **fraction** is simply $\frac{20}{100} = \frac{1}{5}$.
>
> The **ratio** of the number of employees leaving to the average number of employees is 20:100 or **1:5**.

Practice Questions

Q1 Why can graphs and charts sometimes be misleading?

Q2 Explain the difference between the "mean", "median" and "mode" of a set of data.

Q3 What do index numbers show?

Exam Questions

Q1 Discuss how statistics can hinder as well as help decision-making.

Answer on p.107. [8 marks]

Q2 Look back at the revenue table for the Italian restaurant on page 99. The restaurant owners now decide to take 2012 as their base year. Calculate the new revenue index for 2014. [2 marks]

Ladies and gentlemen, you have been warned — maths kills...

All this maths stuff can be very helpful, but it can also be biased. If you're given a table or graph as part of an exam question, watch out for things like how the axes are labelled, whether the axes start at zero, and whether important info is left out. Businesses often use graphs and charts to put their facts and figures in as good a light as possible.

The AS Exams

This page will get you familiar with how the AS exams are set out, so when you turn up on the day, you'll know exactly what to expect from each paper.

These pages are for AS Business. If you're doing the full A level, you'll have your exams at the end of the course.

The **AS Level** has **Two Exam Papers**

1) AS Business is made up of **two exams** — Paper 1 (Business 1) and Paper 2 (Business 2).

2) Both exams test the **whole AS course** — that's everything in sections 1-6 of this book. They also test your **maths skills** — calculating and interpreting data crops up in different topics, and there are some more general maths skills you need as well (see section 7).

3) The two exams don't have exactly the same **style** of questions — so practise answering the different types of questions that can come up.

4) Each exam lasts for **1 hour 30 minutes** and is worth **80 marks**. Allowing for reading time, that means you need to achieve a **mark almost every minute**. Each paper counts for **50%** of your AS level.

5) Each paper tests the same four **assessment objectives** (AOs). These are AO1 (**showing knowledge**), AO2 (**applying knowledge**), AO3 (**analysis**) and AO4 (**evaluation**) — there's more detail on each AO on the next page. The AOs have **different weightings** on each paper (see below).

At least 10% of the exam marks will be for maths skills.

Paper 1 has **Three Different Sections**

Paper 1 is made up of **three different sections** — Section A is worth **10 marks**, Section B is worth about **20 marks** and Section C is worth about **50 marks**. Each section is made up of different **types** of question.

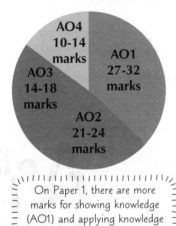

AO4 10-14 marks
AO1 27-32 marks
AO3 14-18 marks
AO2 21-24 marks

On Paper 1, there are more marks for showing knowledge (AO1) and applying knowledge (AO2) than for the other AOs.

1) Section **A** is made up of **10 multiple choice questions**, worth **1 mark** each. There are 4 options to choose from for each question.

2) Section **B** is made up of about **4 short-answer questions**, worth around **4-6 marks** each (though this may vary). You'll need to **cover a few points** in these answers, or show a few steps of working in **calculation** questions.

3) In Section **C**, you'll be given **two mini case studies** and asked questions on them (these are known as **data response questions**). The questions on each case study are worth **25 marks** in total — there could be **2 or 3 questions** on each one. These questions need **extended answers** and so are worth more marks.

Paper 2 asks questions about a **Case Study**

For Paper 2, you'll be given a **case study** and asked **questions** about it.

1) In the **case study**, you'll be given some information about a **business**. There will usually be some **written information** and some **data** (e.g. costs or profits).

2) You'll be asked roughly **7 or 8 questions** on the case study, ranging from **short-answer questions** (worth around **3-4 marks**) to **extended-answer questions** (worth **16 or 20 marks**).

3) The extended-answer questions tend to come towards the **end** of the paper, so make sure you leave enough **time** for them.

4) Some of the questions will involve **calculations** and **interpretation** based on the data you've been given.

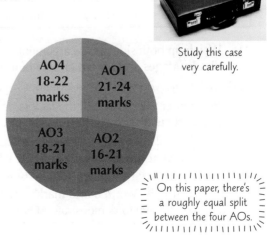

Study this case very carefully.

AO4 18-22 marks
AO1 21-24 marks
AO3 18-21 marks
AO2 16-21 marks

On this paper, there's a roughly equal split between the four AOs.

Get Marks in Your AS Exams

These pages explain how the exams are marked. Basically, the marks are divided up into four different skills — AO1, AO2, AO3 and AO4. So to get all the marks, you need to demonstrate all the skills.

You get marks for *Showing Knowledge (AO1)* and *Applying Knowledge (AO2)*

AO1 and AO2 questions usually start with words like "**Describe**", "**Explain**" or "**Calculate**".

"**Describe**" questions ask you to say what something **shows** or **means**, "**explain**" means you have to **give reasons** for something and "**calculate**" means you have to **work something out**.

1) **AO1** marks are for **content** and **knowledge** of e.g. **terms**, **methods** and **theories**.
2) This means things like knowing the **proper definitions** for **business terms** (this is often what you're asked for in **multiple choice** questions).
3) For a multiple choice question, you'll get **1 mark** for AO1. For longer questions, you'll usually get between **2-4 marks** for AO1, whether the question is a **short-answer** one worth 4 marks, or an **extended-answer** one worth 16 marks.

> To make sure you get marks for content, always give definitions of terms you're using, or formulas if you're doing a calculation.

1) **AO2** marks are for **application** — applying your knowledge to a situation. This means thinking about the **type of business** in the **question**, the product or service it's selling, and the type of market it's in.
2) Numerical **calculations** and **interpretation** are also awarded **application** marks.
3) AO2 is usually worth **2-3 marks**, but questions which want you to demonstrate AO2 will be expecting you to demonstrate **AO1** too, so they'll be worth between **4 and 6 marks** overall.

You'll get more marks when you *Analyse (AO3)* and *Evaluate (AO4)*

AO3 marks are for **analysis** — thinking about benefits, drawbacks, influences, effects and limitations.

Analysis questions often start with the word "**Analyse**".

1) Use your knowledge to **explain** your answer and give **reasons**.
2) If there's data, say what the figures **mean**, talk about what might have **caused** them and say what **effect** you think they will have on the business in the **future**.
3) Use **logical reasoning** to link **influences**, **actions** and their **effects** together.
4) Consider **both sides** of the **argument** — you can only get **limited** analysis **marks** by looking at **one side**.
5) AO3 is worth about **3-5 marks** — but the questions will expect you to demonstrate **AO1** and **AO2** (and maybe even **AO4**) as well. AO3 marks are usually given for **longer-answer** questions (worth **9, 16** or **20 marks**).

Lucinda, Tarquin, Jemima and Angelica were experts at demonstrating AOs 1-4.

AO4 marks are for **evaluation** — using your **judgement**.

Evaluation questions usually start with words like "**Evaluate**", "**Justify**" or "**To what extent**".

1) **Weigh up** both sides of the argument — consider the **advantages** and **disadvantages** and say which **side** of the argument you think is **strongest**.
2) Make sure you **justify** your opinions — you should always give **evidence** to support your views.
3) Remember to consider **all** the factors involved when you're asked to consider the importance of a **particular factor**. This is essential when answering "**to what extent**" questions.
4) You don't always need a **definite** answer. You can point out that it **depends** on various factors — as long as you say **what the factors are**, and say **why** the right choice depends on those factors. Use your judgement to say what the **most important factors** are. The most important thing is to **justify** what you're saying.
5) AO4 is usually worth **6** or **8 marks**. It's tested in **extended-answer** questions (worth **16** or **20 marks**) and you'll have to demonstrate **AOs 1-3** in these questions as well.

Get Marks in Your AS Exams

Make sure you write *Clearly* and *Structure* your answers well

1) You have to use the **right style** of writing and **arrange relevant information clearly** — write in **full sentences** and **link** your points together. Don't just write a list of bullet points. You need to use **specialist vocabulary** when it's appropriate, so it's well worth **learning** the **fancy terms** used in this book.

2) You have to write **neatly** enough for the examiner to be able to read it. You also need to use good **spelling**, **grammar** and **punctuation** to make your meaning **crystal clear**. Don't worry, you won't lose marks for spelling errors — but if your handwriting, grammar, spelling and punctuation are **so** far up the spout that the examiner **can't understand** what you've written, **expect problems**.

3) You won't get any marks for **written communication** — but you might **lose marks** if the examiner can't **read** or **understand** your writing.

Jotting down a quick plan will help with extended-answer questions.

Dudley got no marks for his "Boston Matrix in Mime".

The *Examiner* will try to show you *How Much to Write*

1) The examiner does try to help you by telling you how many **marks** each question is worth and by giving you an idea of how **much** you need to write. The **more lines** there are for an answer, the **more** you're expected to **write**.

2) Remember, you're aiming to score **a mark a minute** — so if a question is worth **5 marks**, you should spend about **5 minutes** on it.

3) Generally, if the question is worth **2 or 3 marks** then you just need to show your business **knowledge**. Give a **short answer** and move on quickly.

4) For a **16** or **20 mark** question, you need to show **analysis** and **evaluation**. You'll have to write much more for these questions. They usually expect you to make a **decision**, or have an **opinion** and be able to **justify** it. There's rarely a right or wrong answer to this sort of question, so just **convince** the examiner that your opinion is **valid** by **explaining** your reasons.

Don't forget to include *All* the *Skills* in *Extended-Answer Questions*

1) When you come up against a long question (worth, say, 16 marks), **don't jump** straight to the **evaluation** stage. The examiner will be looking for **evidence** of the **other skills**, too.

2) Remember, a question testing **AO4** will also be testing **AOs 1-3** — so you need to demonstrate **all** of the assessment objectives (see previous page).

3) So, if they ask you how a business can increase its profits, and you think it should either decrease its **operating expenses** or make some staff **redundant**, you need to:

> 1) **Define** what is meant by operating expenses and redundancy (this will get you your **AO1** marks).
>
> 2) Explain how operating expenses/redundancy are **relevant** to the type of **business** in the question (for **AO2** marks).
>
> 3) Give the **advantages** and **disadvantages** of each method of increasing profits (for **AO3** marks).
>
> 4) Finally, for the **AO4** marks, **weigh up** both sides of the argument and **decide** if the business should decrease its operating expenses or make some staff redundant (you might decide it needs to do both).

For an example of an extended answer, which demonstrates all the skills, see p.105.

It's exam time — let's get down to business...

These pages should take some of the surprise out of your exams. You don't need to know this upside down and back to front like you do the actual business stuff. What you do need to know is what the examiners actually want to see from you — not <u>just</u> that you know the facts, but also that you understand and can use what you've learnt.

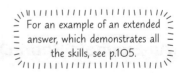

Worked Exam Questions

Here's an example of the kind of case study and questions you might get in Paper 2.

Crinkle Cakes Ltd

Crinkle Cakes Ltd is a business that makes cakes, set up by Janet Jones, who made cakes in her own kitchen to sell to family and friends. Over eight years, it has grown from a sole trader business to a medium-sized private limited company. Although Ms Jones still plays an important day-to-day role in the business, it is no longer based in her kitchen. The business now operates out of premises equipped with machinery which allows them to produce 50 cakes per hour. Crinkle Cakes employs 40 staff on both full-time and part-time contracts.

The business operates in a very competitive market which is dominated by two national bakeries. It also faces competition from a long-established local firm, which has an excellent reputation in the area. In order to ensure the long-term survival of the business, Crinkle Cakes needs to compete more effectively and achieve its objective of increasing both sales and market share. Money is tight though, since the machinery was obtained using a bank loan which is still being paid off.

Crinkle Cakes aims to sell its products in the big supermarkets, but so far has been unable to secure a deal to supply any of the major chains. The main reasons the supermarkets gave for not stocking Crinkle Cakes products were that they had a very narrow product range (selling only whole cakes rather than multi-pack slices or individual portions), and that their cakes were priced higher than competing bakeries.

The marketing manager has been looking at ways to expand the product range. He did some market research into the types of cakes consumers buy, and the results are displayed below (see Table 1). He also examined the prices of the cakes in their market. Crinkle Cakes had originally aimed to charge prices that could compete with the local competitor, but the reality is that Crinkle Cakes's prices are on average 10% higher than their local competitor's and approximately 30% higher than the national competitors'. The marketing manager wants to decrease the price of their cakes, but to do this the company will have to cut costs.

The operations manager has been looking at ways to cut costs. She has discovered that one problem is the rising cost of ingredients from their suppliers. Table 2 shows the expenditure budget and their actual expenditure for a typical month.

Table 1
Results from Market Research (Percentage of People Asked)

Product	Purchased weekly	Purchased monthly	Purchased rarely	Never purchased
Whole cakes	2	8	62	28
Multi-pack, e.g. slices	55	23	14	8
Individual portions	67	17	10	6

Table 2
Expenditure Budget

	Budget	Actual	Variance
Raw materials	£20k	£30k	£10k (A)
Staff costs	£50k	£48k	£2k (F)
Marketing	£5k	£8k	£3k (A)
Insurance & utility bills	£10k	£8k	£2k (F)
Other	£5k	£4k	£1k (F)

An *Example Short Question and Answer* to give you some tips:

Q1 Crinkle Cakes Ltd is a private limited company.
Explain **two** features of the legal structure of Crinkle Cakes Ltd. (4 marks)

Crinkle Cakes is owned by its shareholders, who have bought shares privately. The shares cannot be bought by the public and won't be quoted on a stock exchange.
The shareholders of Crinkle Cakes have limited liability, which means that they are not personally responsible for the debts of the business. The only money they can lose is the money they have invested in the company.

Other points that could have been made include the fact that Crinkle Cakes doesn't have a minimum share capital requirement and that a shareholder will need the agreement of other shareholders to sell their shares.

Worked Exam Questions

An *Example Extended Question and Answer* to give you some tips:

Q2 Crinkle Cakes Ltd are considering changing their marketing mix to make the business more competitive.
To what extent do you think that the product is the most important element of the mix to change? (16 marks)

Stating knowledge is fine, but don't waste too much time on it

AO1: Refers to, and defines, marketing mix

The marketing mix is all the factors a business has to take into account when marketing a product. This is more commonly referred to as "the seven Ps" of product, price, place, promotion, people, physical environment and process. In order to adapt a marketing mix it is necessary to examine each of these factors in turn.

AO2: Links knowledge about marketing mix to business in question

Make use of information in the case study

AO3: Identifies problems and suggests solutions

Apply your suggestions to the business in question

AO4: Evaluates the impact of changes to the product

There are a number of ways in which Crinkle Cakes could make changes to the product. At present they produce mainly whole cakes, which 28% of customers never buy according to the research findings in Table 1. This has meant that few supermarkets have shown a willingness to sell Crinkle Cakes' products. Based on this, one change would be to make a wider range of cake sizes. In addition to the whole cakes, they could introduce a multi-pack containing cake slices, aimed at families, and single-slice packs, perhaps aimed at single people or impulse buyers. This would increase the market segments they appeal to and increase the likelihood of sales to the big supermarkets. Another alteration that Crinkle Cakes could make to their products is to target niche markets (e.g. by making gluten-free products), which would reduce their competition and would mean that they could charge higher prices and still be competitive. However, this may require further market research.

AO2: Links issue of price to business in question

AO3: Identifies problems and suggests solutions

AO4: Evaluates the impact of changes to the price

Make use of information in the case study

Another element of the marketing mix is price. The case study states that Crinkle Cakes charges higher prices than its competitors, but that this is necessary because of costs, e.g. of ingredients. Table 2 shows that they are paying £10K per month more for their raw materials than budgeted, which will impact on costs and the prices they can charge. To be able to charge more competitive prices, Crinkle Cakes could cut costs, e.g. by negotiating a better deal with their supplier, or by changing suppliers. Lower prices would make the cakes more appealing to consumers and especially the big supermarkets. Or, instead of trying to reduce prices, the company could market the cakes as a luxury item (or aimed at a particular niche market) to justify the prices.

This is a little vague

Here you could refer to Table 2, which shows an adverse variance for marketing costs that could limit changes to promotion

AO3: Links marketing decisions with actions

As far as place is concerned, Crinkle Cakes could take steps to get their products into the major supermarkets, which should be possible if they make the changes to the product size already discussed. Crinkle Cakes could also attempt to supply high-end bakeries if they decide to sell luxury cakes.

The case study does not give any detail about what promotion has taken place. The company could reposition their brand as a luxury cake company in order to differentiate themselves from their competitors. They could also consider promoting their products through a company website or social media to increase awareness and demand.

This is too brief

AO4: Makes vague attempt at overall analysis

There is very little information in the case study about the people, physical environment and process of Crinkle Cakes, so it is not possible to recommend how to improve these factors.

In conclusion, adapting the product is very important to the continued success of Crinkle Cakes, but there are other factors that need to change too.

- This is a reasonably good answer and would get about **12 marks**. It considers a range of changes to the marketing mix and applies them to the business in the case study. This answer has been set out sensibly with a separate paragraph for each aspect of the marketing mix.

- However, it doesn't use the information given in Table 2 when talking about promotion, and the last three Ps have been skimmed over. Although there isn't much information in the case study, it would have been good to make **suggestions** on how to use these factors to increase competitiveness.

- The **conclusion** is poor and doesn't add anything to the answer. It doesn't really answer the question, and doesn't cover the 'to what extent' element of the question.

Answers to Numerical Questions

Page 7 — Exam Questions

Q1   Total costs = 23 + 54 = 77% of revenue *[1 mark]*
So profit = 100 – 77 = 23% of revenue *[1 mark]*
23% of £650 000 = £149 500 *[1 mark]*

Q2   a)

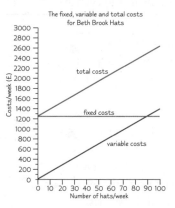

The fixed, variable and total costs for Beth Brook Hats

[6 marks available — 1 mark for each correct start/finish point of each line]

b)   Costs at 60 hats per week
= fixed costs + variable costs *[1 mark]*
= 1260 + (60 × 14) = £1260 + £840
= £2100 *[1 mark]*
Revenue = selling price × quantity sold
= £50 × 60 = £3000 *[1 mark]*
Profit = revenue – costs = £3000 – £2100
= £900 *[1 mark]*

Page 23 — Exam Question

Q1   a)

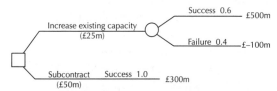

[4 marks available — 1 mark for two branches for the courses of action, 1 mark for the correct probabilities for increasing existing capacity, 1 mark for the correct pay-offs for increasing existing capacity, 1 mark for the correct probability and pay-off for subcontracting]

b)   Expected value of increasing existing capacity:
(0.6 × 500m) + (0.4 × –100m) *[1 mark]*
= 300m – 40m *[1 mark]* = £260m *[1 mark]*
Net gain = £260m – £25m = £235m *[1 mark]*
Expected value of subcontracting:
1.0 × 300m *[1 mark]* = £300m *[1 mark]*
Net gain = £300m – £50m = £250m *[1 mark]*
Based on the decision tree, the company should subcontract *[1 mark]*

Page 29 — Exam Questions

Q1   a)   If they increase their 2013 sales by 10% they will sell:
(250 × 10%) + 250 = 275 units *[1 mark]*
They actually sold 290 units in 2014 so they have met their objective. *[1 mark]*

Page 33 — Exam Question

Q1   a)

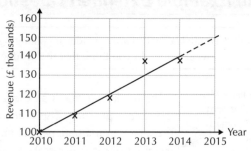

So in 2015 the estimated revenue is £150 000.

[3 marks available — 1 mark for drawing a line of best fit, 1 mark for extrapolating your line to 2015, 1 mark for reading the value from your graph correctly]

Page 37 — Exam Questions

Q1   The company's current revenue is
£1500 × 200 = £300 000 *[1 mark]*

Price elasticity of demand
$$= \frac{\% \text{ change in quantity demanded}}{\% \text{ change in price}}$$ *[1 mark]*

So, % change in quantity demanded
= price elasticity of demand × % change in price
= –0.7 × 15% = –10.5% *[1 mark]*

The new price of a horse will be
£1500 + (£1500 × 15%) = £1725 *[1 mark]*

100 – 10.5 = 89.5%
The company will sell
200 × 89.5% = 179 horses *[1 mark]*

The company's new revenue will be
179 × £1725 = £308 775 *[1 mark]*

Which is an increased revenue of
£308 775 – £300 000 = £8775 *[1 mark]*

Page 57 — Practice Questions

Q1   Capacity utilisation (%) $= \dfrac{\text{output}}{\text{capacity}} \times 100$

$= \dfrac{44}{64} \times 100 = 68.75\%$

Q3   Unit cost $= \dfrac{\text{total costs}}{\text{units output}} = \dfrac{£1719}{450} = £3.82$

Page 57 — Exam Question

Q1   a)   Weekly capacity = 7 × 3 × 300
= 6300 *[1 mark]*

Capacity utilisation (%) $= \dfrac{\text{output}}{\text{capacity}} \times 100$

$= \dfrac{2205}{6300} \times 100$ *[1 mark]*

$= 35\%$ *[1 mark]*

Answers to Numerical Questions

Page 59 — Practice Questions

Q1 Output per hour = 168 000 ÷ 35 = 4800 m²

Labour productivity = $\dfrac{\text{output per period}}{\text{number of employees}}$

$= \dfrac{4800}{4}$

= 1200 m² per worker per hour

So the correct option is C.

Page 64 — Practice Questions

Q3 Re-order level = lead time × average daily usage
                    + buffer stock level

= 5 × 9 + 7 = 52 units

Page 64 — Exam Question

Q1

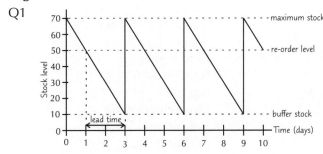

[4 marks available — 1 mark for the correct maximum and buffer stock, 1 mark for the correct reorder level, 1 mark for the correct lead time and 1 mark for the black line drawn correctly]

Page 71 — Practice Questions

Q1 Percentage change in profit

$= \dfrac{\text{current year's profit} - \text{previous year's profit}}{\text{previous year's profit}} \times 100$

$= \dfrac{52\,000 - 50\,000}{50\,000} \times 100 = \dfrac{2000}{50\,000} \times 100 = 4\%$

Q2 Profit for the year = operating profit + other profit
    − net finance costs − tax
    = £21 000 + £3000 − £2000 − £6000
    = £16 000

Page 71 — Exam Questions

Q2 a) Operating profit = sales revenue − cost of sales
        − operating expenses
        = gross profit − operating expenses *[1 mark]*
        = £750 000 − £250 000 = £500 000 *[1 mark]*

Operating profit margin (%)

$= \dfrac{\text{operating profit}}{\text{sales revenue}} \times 100$ *[1 mark]*

$= \dfrac{£500\,000}{£2\,000\,000} \times 100 = 25\%$ *[1 mark]*

Page 73 — Practice Questions

Q3 Net cash flow = cash inflows − cash outflows
                 = £8000 − £9500 = (£1500)

Q4 Closing balance = opening balance + net cash flow
                    = £20 000 + (£7000) = £13 000

Page 75 — Practice Questions

Q2 Profit budget = income budget − expenditure budget
    Rearranging gives:
    Expenditure budget = income budget − profit budget
    = £125 000 − £30 000 = £95 000

Page 77 — Practice Questions

Q2 Variance = £15 000 − £18 000 = £3000 (A)
    so there is a £3000 adverse variance.

Page 77 — Exam Question

Q1 a)

	Feb cumulative variance	Mar budget	Mar actual	Mar variance	Mar cumulative variance
Revenue	£10k (A)	£110k	£120k	£10k (F)	£0
Wages	£9k (F)	£40k	£39k	£1k (F)	£10k (F)
Rent	£1k (A)	£10k	£11k	£1k (A)	£2k (A)
Other costs	£2k (A)	£5k	£5k	£0	£2k (A)
Total costs	£6k (F)	£55k	£55k	£0	£6k (F)

[10 marks available — 1 mark for each of the variances in red]

Page 79 — Exam Questions

Q2 Contribution per unit =
    selling price per unit − variable costs per unit
    [1 mark]
    = £13 − £5 = £8 *[1 mark]*

Break-even output $= \dfrac{\text{fixed costs}}{\text{contribution per unit}}$ *[1 mark]*

$= \dfrac{£1000}{£8} = 125$ customers *[1 mark]*

Page 85 — Practice Questions

Q2 Labour cost per unit $= \dfrac{\text{labour costs}}{\text{units of output}}$

Labour costs = units of output × labour cost per unit
             = 50 × £100 = £5000

Q4 Labour Turnover (%)

$= \dfrac{\text{number of staff leaving}}{\text{average number of staff employed}} \times 100$

$= \dfrac{18}{600} \times 100 = 3\%$

Page 100 — Exam Questions

Q2 Divide revenue of 2014 by the revenue of
    the base year (2012) and multiply by 100:

$\dfrac{24650}{21250} \times 100$ *[1 mark]* = 116 *[1 mark]*

Index

Index

Index